These Moorhouse Lectures, delivered in Melbourne in 1973, are concerned with the relationship of moral insights to human institutions and with the way in which notoriously unfaithful man can show moral fidelity. Ethics, Professor Dunstan argues, require skilled workmanship, which is why ethics may be termed an artifice. The work of the craftsman in morals is to take a vision and realize it: his work is not done until he has transcribed his vision into the structure of a social institution. Posterity may misuse the institution, but that does not invalidate the need for moral insight to be woven into the fabric of a society. Conventions are needed which embody fidelity, because of the dangers of human infidelity, though in a rapidly changing situation, new conventions are always needed.

This argument, and the questions raised by it, sets the pattern for the chapters which follow. Professor Dunstan considers the relationship between insight and institutions in the Bible and in the church. He then goes on to consider the contribution and authority of the moralist in particular areas: there is a full discussion of medical ethics, and abortion and euthanasia are given special attention. Finally, he considers how international self-interest may be mastered in the service of conventions embodying trust, with special discussion of the limitation of nuclear, chemical and bacteriological weapons.

Gordon Dunstan is Professor of Moral and Social Theology at King's College, University of London.

The Artifice of Ethics

G. R. DUNSTAN

The Artifice of Ethics

The Moorhouse Lectures 1973

SCM PRESS LTD

334 00060 2

First published 1974
by SCM Press Ltd
56 Bloomsbury Street, London
© SCM Press Ltd 1974

Printed in Great Britain by
Northumberland Press Ltd
Gateshead

Contents

Foreword

A book by Professor Gordon Dunstan needs no foreword or recommendation. He has put the Church of England, and indeed many outside the Church of England, in his debt for his writings on moral theology, either anonymously through the Board for Social Responsibility of the Church of England, or through the introduction which he wrote for the 1958 Lambeth Conference on the Family in Contemporary Society.

We in Australia are starved theologically; there is no single professorial chair of theology anywhere in this country. It was therefore to our great pleasure and profit that Professor Dunstan was able to accept our invitation to be the Moorhouse Lecturer in August 1973. It happened that just at that time, and during the previous twelve months, Australian society had been wracked with controversy on moral issues, and Professor Dunstan's lectures, which are here reproduced, were not only timely for those who heard them, but provided just that strong Christian background of thought which we very much needed; and his knowledge added to the weight of authority both of the lectures and of the answers given in discussion.

This book makes available to a wide public the privilege had by those who listened to the lectures. They should be read, marked, learned and inwardly digested by Christians interested in these moral problems, and that must surely be most Christians everywhere.

FRANK WOODS   *January 1974*
Archbishop of Melbourne
Primate of the Church of England in Australia

Preface

I am indebted to the Archbishop of Melbourne, the Most Reverend Frank Woods, KBE, for the honour of his invitation to deliver the Moorhouse Lectures in 1973, a characteristic expression of that generous friendship of his which I have enjoyed since I served as his assistant curate at Huddersfield Parish Church nearly thirty years ago. With him I would thank the Warden of Trinity College, Melbourne, Dr Robin Sharwood, for his sensitive hospitality to my wife and me during our visit, and the officers of the Trinity School of Theology and the United Faculty of Theology in the University of Melbourne which together assured a lively and responsive audience for the lectures.

Others who entertained us so agreeably, in church and university, during our long journey to, through and from the antipodes are too many to name; together they set the Moorhouse Lectures in a girdle of experience rich in contrast, in challenge to peripheral beliefs and in confirmation of fundamental ones. To them also, and to those whom they brought together to hear and discourse with us, more than formal thanks are due: in Auckland, Rotorua, Palmerston North and Wellington; in Christchurch and Dunedin; in Melbourne, Sydney, Townsville, Rockhampton, Brisbane, Canberra, Perth; in Bangkok; in Calcutta with the Oxford Mission, in Ranchi with the blind at St Michael's School, in Kamdara and Delhi; and, last of all, in Isfahan where, coming only with the expectations of tourists relaxing after a journey not without its demands, we were taken into the heart of a missionary enterprise of evident spiritual power.

As a Western industrialized Christian of the sort to be found anywhere in England, North America, Australia or New Zealand, I still recall the quickening surprise with which I recognized, in the poverty of Calcutta and Chota Nagpur and in the articulate missionary church in Iran, Christianity of an authenticity to which I was becoming a stranger. I call it authentic because, without *alias* or anonymity, it lives by the integration of worship and witness with the diligent service of needy men; because those who serve in the schools, the hospitals, the training centres and the crowded streets still think it natural to name the name of the deliverer, the Christ crucified and glorified, the Christ in those whom they serve. The church door open, the bell, the people there, the primacy of liturgy and prayer, even the white habits in the streets, speak the name of the author and finisher of their work. To have experienced this, familiar, of course, to other travellers and axiomatic to missionary Christians themselves, was an enrichment more than the Moorhouse Lecturer could ever have expected, but for which, with so much besides, he is profoundly grateful.

The third lecture originated in a paper prepared for the Anglican-Roman Catholic International Commission, and it has been developed and printed with permission. The others have grown out of the constraints put upon a teacher.

King's College, London   *G. R. D.*
The Epiphany, 1974

I

Community and Convention

'If the whole dead weight of sin were ever to be allowed to fall upon the law, it could never take the strain.' Lord Devlin spoke those words, in his celebrated Maccabaean Lecture of the British Academy in 1958 on 'Morals and the Criminal Law'. I am not at all sure that the church and its moral theologians have ever taken them as seriously as they ought to be taken. They occur at the end of the lecture, in a summary of its main contention:

> What is the relationship between crime and sin, between the Church and the Law? I do not think that you can equate crime with sin. The divine law and the secular have been disunited, but they are brought together again by the need which each has for the other. It is not my function to emphasize the Church's need of the secular law; it can be put tersely by saying that you cannot have a ceiling without a floor. I am very clear about the law's need for the Church. I have spoken of the criminal law as dealing with minimum standards of human conduct and the moral law with the maximum. The instrument of the criminal law is punishment; those of the moral law are teaching, training, and exhortation. If the whole dead weight of sin were ever to be allowed to fall upon the law, it could not take the strain. If at any point there is a lack of clear and convincing moral teaching, the administration of the law suffers.

The lecture ended with the words, 'Without the help of Christian teaching the law will fail.'[1]

It may fairly be observed, I think, that these words have not been taken seriously because Christian preoccupation, in the last fifteen years, has been in other directions. In terms of the domestic argument in which Lord Devlin was engaged, the relationship between morals and the criminal law, the more vocal interpretations of Christian ethics have been individualistic, emphasizing the moral freedom of the individual and of his personal, day-to-day decision, to the neglect of the common

morality or corporate interest of the community, whether of
church or human society. The strength of vocal, liberal, Christian support for the reform of the law on homosexual offences
and abortion, for instance, would have surprised an earlier generation. This individualism in local, personal morality has been
accompanied by a passionate concern to right social wrongs far
away – racialism in southern Africa, economic domination in
the Americas, and the relief of poverty and hunger the world
over. So we live in paradox. Individualism in personal morality
has tended, on the whole, to offer freedom from guilt, not by
the word of forgiveness, but by formulae of justification, in the
language of situationism in its various forms, of 'the most loving' or 'the most compassionate' thing to do. Social concern, on
the other hand, literally trades in guilt: it lays the burden of
responsibility for the world's ills on Christian people whose
only offence, most of them, is to live in an industrialized society
whose corporate potential for growing richer far exceeds that of
the poorer countries, and which undoubtedly used and exploited
those countries to make its own industrial expansion more
rapid. The guilty conscience of Christians in the industrialized
countries today over social and economic conditions for which
only the tiniest few of them have ever had actual personal
responsibility – and therefore even the possibility of moral fault
– is not a whit less than the sense of guilt which pervaded the
Reformation liturgies or the hymns and piety of the Evangelical
Revival. And this sense of guilt is exploited, partly to raise
money for Christian Aid and the rest, partly to provoke to a
largely ineffectual anger against 'the system' and 'the structures'
which appear to frustrate all attempts at reform.

Lord Devlin argues that the moral cohesion of a community –
which is essential to its survival – cannot be maintained by the
coercive force of law alone: secular restraints are not enough to
deter from evil, or even from anti-social or merely illegal acts; we
need the conscientious determination and effort of citizens to
maintain morality and to uphold the law; otherwise law enforcement becomes tyrannical and remains impossible even so. We
cannot do without a sense of guilt. Moral individualism of the
sort now in vogue tends to deny the community the assurance
of that support; it atomizes morality, isolating each individual
and each decision from its context in society and moral con-

tinuity. 'Love' for the nearest neighbour, the one claiming 'compassion' at any moment of time – whether compounded or not with love for the self, and for whatever personal feeling is part of the 'compassion' – is advanced at the expense of the neighbour unknown and further away, the neighbour whose security is threatened by the erosion of moral community.

The distant social concern, on the other hand, is not well served by the exploitation of guilt. It is axiomatic in theology that loving acts among men are responses to the proclaimed and experienced love of God. The wrath of men does not work the purposes of God; and good works spring from grace, not from guilt. The structures of world finance and trade, and their political undergirding, show themselves to be particularly unshakable by demonstrations of righteous anger and moralist assault. Yet they must be changed if the poor are to be served. If they persist too long unchanged, they will probably be overthrown – first over-complicated to the point of strangulation by perpetual self-defence against competitive self-interest within; then the more easily destroyed by war or revolution from without. The process is well documented in the Bible and in history, and is known theologically as 'judgment'. But that fate is not inevitable. It can be averted by reformation from within; and reformation can be accompanied by men seeking to achieve their moral purpose – the working out of the obligation of love in the service of the needy and of the common good – by men possessed both of the Gospel of hope and of the necessary technical competence – and hence the necessary positions of trust – within the relevant economic, financial and political fields.

At present, then, in the personal diagnosis which I venture to make, Western Christian moral attitudes are not conspicuously effective in either area of activity, the maintenance of a moral base in the local community or the outreach of service to the under-privileged and oppressed. If this be so, it may be because the dominant or more forcefully articulated moral theories are at fault. In reaction from individualism I experiment – and in full awareness of the dangers which I run of being both mistaken and misunderstood – I experiment with the language of *convention*.

My theme is the *artifice* of ethics. *Artificium* is skilled workmanship, wrought in obedience to the discipline proper to the art. Ethics requires such workmanship of man the *artifex*, the moral craftsman disciplined by and for a divine and human art. His art is, sometimes, to produce as a musician produces a lovely sound, heard for a moment and then lost; but more commonly to transcribe his sound – whether heard yet, or still only imagined – into music and write it down, that others and posterity may have it and hear it for ever. So the moralist has his moment of vision; he may utter what he sees, in a word of compelling force; and he may be listened to, or not. But his work is not done until he has transcribed his vision into the structure of a social institution, to last when his words are no longer heard but forgotten. Posterity may misuse the institution, just as later performers of the music may perform it ill; that hazard will be determined by the quality of another institution, the tradition of musical skill handed on by conductors and musicians from generation to generation. But the composer has done his work when he has transcribed his musical vision with integrity; without his artifice, there can be no art. The point which I seek to establish is so important that I beg to multiply my metaphors. The moralist, having seen his vision, or arrived at his position by moral reasoning, must weave his insight into the fabric of society by creating an institution in which to embody it; or, having floated his boat on a rising tide up on to the beach, must secure it there against the ebb, and wait for another tide, it may be, to carry it higher. That institutions may be abused – that anchors may drag, or sands may shift and estuaries may change their tides – are hazards against which he may guard but which he cannot control; they do not excuse him from his duty. And it is precisely for this neglect of or disdain for the social institutions in which moral insights are embodied that contemporary moralists – or at least the moralizing church – may come most to be censured. No so some among the philosophers: Dorothy Emmet, in *Rules, Roles and Relations*,[2] and R. S. Downie and Elizabeth Telfer in *Respect for Persons*[3] and R. S. Downie alone in *Roles and Values*[4] have insisted on the institutional dimension of ethics; and the voice of jurisprudence through Lord Devlin we have already heard. The bias or tendency of these lectures is by design upon this side.

The institutions by means of which moral insights are embodied and carried in a society are many and various. The one with which Lord Devlin was concerned was the criminal law, but that is not the only one. The church, with its moral tradition, is another; and particular churches vary in the degree to which they back their moral tradition with the sanctions of a canon law or corporate discipline. The professions, with their codes of ethics and disciplinary procedures, stand high in my list of moral institutions, and they will be found to have more than a passing reference in these lectures. There are also countless voluntary societies in which, beneath or attending the sheer fellowship, there is a bond of association of a moral sort: Scouting and Guiding have an international status, with a simple but authentic moral code; Youth Hostelling, International Voluntary Service, Voluntary Service Overseas and the like all embody a general set of moral ideals, with an evident appeal to men and women of student age, and develop internal codes of conduct for themselves, necessary for the harmonious working of local communities or groups. An older generation has Toc H, the British Legion and other veterans' associations, the Women's Institute, Townswomen's Guilds, Rotary Clubs, Soroptimists and the Mothers' Union, each embodying a characteristic moral view within its bond of association, though varying from others, of course, in the degree and frequency of its articulating the moral element over against the practical or social.

Now if we look for one word with which to designate the sort of moral control exercised both within these institutions, professional as well as social, and by them upon society as a whole, I suggest that we may find it in *conventions*. It is with the place of the *convention* in the community that this lecture is chiefly concerned. And my intention in developing it is not to declare what ought to be, or how we ought to behave, but to recall, from common experience, what in fact is, how in fact we do behave. My hope is that when we recognize a little more clearly the moral imperatives by which, without much explicit or self-conscious use of moral language, we live together, we shall realize more the importance of these imperatives in the life of a community and may indeed wish to strengthen them.

I use the word 'community' with a floating relevance, to cover a variety of associations. It presupposes that the life natural and proper to man is one in ordered relationships of various sorts; that whenever men have to do things together they create social organizations in which to do them. We tend to give these the name 'community' only when they are of a satisfying sort, when the relationships within the organization do more for the members than merely to fulfil its economic or other direct purpose, by giving personal satisfaction as well. In contrast with such words as 'mob', 'rabble', 'ghetto', 'bedlam', 'prison-house' ('shades of') or 'rat-race', the word 'community' has tones of ethical approval built into it. Were this not so, human life would be less highly adapted to survival than, say, the life of colonies of gulls. (I grant that within the 'ghetto', say, a strong community life, highly moral, cohesive and satisfying, can arise, the stronger for the fact of restriction or persecution; this indeed witnesses to the capacity to bring good out of evil; but the overtone of evil is built into the word 'ghetto' because of our moral belief that men ought not to be forcibly restricted or persecuted in this way; association should be free.) I apply the word 'community', then, with varying degrees of aptness, to the several units of human association which, whatever their economic or material foundation, provide basic human satisfactions and within which ethical questions arise and ethical relationships are sustained: it may be the family, the school, the village or neighbourhood; it may be an industrial or commercial undertaking; or the nation itself. The word could be used – as 'fraternity' is sometimes used – of a closely-knit profession, even though its members are dispersed: for instance, of the law, or medicine, or teaching, or social work; or of the diplomatic corps in a capital city. It could be used of the church; and, indeed, translated back into New Testament Greek, it becomes theologically charged: the word is *koinonia.*

The word 'convention', in common use, has even wider extremes of meaning. At one extreme is its use in the game of bridge – more than a set of rules, but rather a pattern of signals by which players relate their play together; or in some academic communities to denote customs of alleged but dubious antiquity whose purpose, if ever there was one, has been long forgotten. At the other extreme it can denote a major international agreement designed to keep up minimum standards of international morality or to regulate for safety in the air or at sea. Red Cross conventions on the conduct of war and the treatment of prisoners and the wounded, and United Nations Conventions prohibiting chemical or bacteriological warfare, may also be mentioned; they are the subject of a recent important study by Sydney Bailey, in *Prohibitions and Restraints in War*.[5] These are the products of a rudimentary international community conscience; they are designed to deter and restrain nations from war, and to regulate their conduct, and restrain them from aggravating evil if they go to war. They serve also as a criterion or norm by which to judge and even to condemn conduct which falls below what they prescribe – so that the moral insight, the judgment of *what ought to be*, is preserved for posterity even when one generation has fallen below it. Only some of these have the status of international law; and none is enforceable, without resort to war or other sanctions, because no international court has power at its command to back its jurisdiction. Their status, therefore, is that of a moral agreement or covenant. They embody a moral insight – what ought or ought not to be done, even in war. They are made at a time when there is sufficient goodwill for the moral insight to be accepted multilaterally; and they are made for a time when that goodwill has so diminished or vanished that there is need to limit the harm and destruction done to the community. So we approach the meaning which I give to the word 'convention' for the purpose of this lecture: it is a means of giving stability and permanence to a moral insight by embodying it in an institution, precisely because without the institution it is likely to be lost in time of need.

Conventions are *possible* because men are capable of moral insight, of agreeing in the recognition of moral insight, and of committing themselves to maintain it; they rest on a presupposition of fidelity to a common interest and purpose. Conventions are *necessary* because men fail conspicuously to follow their moral insights and are capable of ruthlessly exploiting one another in the pursuit of self-interest; they rest on a presupposition of infidelity to the community purpose. And in this double statement, of possibility and necessity, stands the realism of ethics – and, incidentally, the realism of Christian theology which sees man as both fallen and free, turned in upon self while still ordained by nature and grace towards community and reconciliation with God.

I offer two observations on the convention in my wider use of the term – that is, leaving aside those few international conventions that have the status of law. The first is that conventions do not rest on the sanctions of the criminal law. The healthier the society, the less it relies upon those sanctions – upon prosecutions, and courts, and punishment. Criminal law exists to secure minimum standards of behaviour essential for the protection of society – a point on which Lord Devlin and Professor Hart[6] agree; it is enforced to restrain conduct destructive of social order and security. The more the law seeks to enforce morality *as such*, without reference to social benefit, cohesion and security (the area of keenest debate between Professor Hart and Lord Devlin), the more intrusive and tyrannical it becomes. The prayer for the temporal power in the old Book of Common Prayer rightly expresses its function: it is 'for the punishment of wickedness and vice', not (as the liberally-intentioned curate would prefer to read it) 'for the *prevention* of wickedness and vice' – that is the church's function, not the law's. The law may properly establish agencies, like the police, for the prevention of crime, and it may include deterrence among the reasons for which it sets penalties for crime, provided that the punishment be not disproportionate to the guilt of the offender; but to ask for the criminal law to prevent wickedness and vice is to ask for tyranny. I shew no disrespect for the law in saying this – and I could say much more about the limitations of law, from the theological tradition as well. The function of law is to guarantee for society that most precious thing, order, and security: there is no state more loveless than anarchy. But life in society is to be lived above law, not by it; even 'working to rule' has now come to mean restrictive working.

My second observation is that conventions lay the emphasis in morals where it ought to be – that morality is first a common possession, a community possession; only secondly, and in the community context, is morality rightly considered as individual choice or decision. This proposition, again, could be argued at length from the theological tradition as from the philosophical; the debate has created its own jargon – 'act-agapeism' and 'rule-agapeism' and the like – as the disputants reconnoitre and contest the field of love.[7] One major office of love is to provide for the continuance of its benefit when the immediate, personal, situational impulse is precisely what is lacking. Love creates relationships, obligations and mutual dependencies which, if they are to endure the vicissitudes of feeling, require institutional embodiment and support: marriage, for instance, in default of perpetual honeymoon. Love must be the parent of justice and equity, among its other protective institutions. But chiefly it begets conventions – possible because men are capable of sociability and fidelity, necessary because they are capable also of exploitation and infidelity. Conventions are the carriers of moral insight, they form the network of moral communication in the community; they provide for moral consistency within a generation and moral continuity for the next. They are related organically to the community's life; so they are not so rigid as to forbid organic change, though they must be firm enough to give the community a moral structure. They operate normally without the intervention of the criminal law; though the final sanction of that law is behind them should their failure threaten the collapse of order. They both demand from men and make possible for them a higher level of morality than the law can enforce; though in a country where parliamentary legislation, the jury system and the tradition of the common law prevail there is always a mutual influence between moral expectations and the judgments of the law.

Conventions embody expectations; they impose limitations; they result in liberation. I would expand these three simple statements in order.

First, expectations. Predictability we take for granted. In the natural sciences, hypotheses are built upon it, and relied upon until falsified; that is to say, once observation has established a regular pattern of behaviour, as, for instance, in the movements of the planets, predictions are made and relied upon; an unexpected departure from the commonly predicted pattern would create a major upheaval in the relevant science. In highly organized industrial societies we rely upon aircraft and trains being available according to time-table; and we reflect on the extent of our reliance only when the services are disorganized by strikes or other hazards. Community life, too, has its established patterns of behaviour: we assume that we know what to expect of one another in roughly comparable situations. A large part of elementary social and moral education consists of training in the meeting of these mutual expectations.

The word *expect* may be used predictively, of the future: 'the lecture is expected to begin at eight o'clock'. But even that simple statement has, built into it, a *prescriptive* sense of expectation: if the lecture is expected to begin at eight o'clock, the lecturer is *expected* to be here, that is, he is under an obligation to be here and you expect him, that is, you morally require him, to meet his obligation. The prescriptive sense – what we prescribe, or say ought to be done – is necessary for the predictive sense – what we expect to happen – to be achieved: the moral obligation is logically prior to the common benefit. So the 'expectation' built into a convention has this double sense, relating obligation to need. Dorothy Emmet, writing with characteristic lucidity in a much-worked area of philosophical debate, puts the matter thus:

> When an obligation is ostensibly being read from the facts of a social situation, this is because a social situation is being understood as a relationship in which certain conduct is expected as appropriate to the roles of the people involved.[8]

Mutual expectation is at the heart of professional ethics. The professional man's conduct is not, in normal situations, regulated from moment to moment by law – though law may prescribe a framework within which his work is done: neither is it at the mercy of his dispositions, how he happens to feel. Society, and his professional colleagues, attach certain expectations to his role: the barrister must defend, in the interest of justice, the most undeserving of criminals; the doctor owes a duty of care to the most unattractive of patients. Expectations may be fluid, or imperfectly understood, in times of rapid social change; but they have a recognizable continuity and cohesion in them. So we create institutions to embody our ethical demands. We embody the ethics of care in the professions of medicine and social work; the concern for justice and equity in the profession of the law; the concern for truth and fidelity in the search for knowledge and in the communicating of it we embody in the professions of academic research and education. We create the profession of accountancy to protect our interest in fair dealing. Business on the Stock Exchange is conducted by conventions designed to secure the maximum freedom of action on the basis of mutual trust; and where trust is imperilled, disciplinary codes are developed to protect it. Fidelity, in this context, means meeting the expectations appropriate to one's role. Personal integrity may often require a man to go beyond them; and always it is necessary to guard against formalism, against meeting the bare formal demand while ignoring or impairing the live, human, ethical reality of the demand behind it.

The expectations are not static: they are raised in response to pressure from the ethical sensitivity of individuals or groups; they are lowered by insensitivity and sloth. They have evolved with our history from our past; but they are by no means a thing of the past. Behind all the talk of permissiveness, behind the demonstrations of anarchy, individual and sectional, there continues a search for security, shewing itself in the framing of new codes of conventions to govern the vital organs of economic, social and political life. In recent months three weighty, separate committees have been at work on codes of ethical practice designed to regulate the conduct of company business, appointed respectively by the Confederation of British Industry, the Institute of Directors and the Institute of Marketing; their reports will be noted in a later lecture. Their work has been done in the context of a keen ethical debate conducted both within the business community itself and under church auspices, notably at St George's House, Windsor Castle; the initiative has been that of the business men; the role of invited churchmen and theologians has been ancillary. In a Britain in the grip of inflation, and threatened with worse, industrial relations and wages negotiations are of critical importance in the pursuit of stability. Mr Wilson's Labour Government intended to regulate the process by law, but abandoned the attempt under pressure from the trade unions. Mr Heath's Conservative Government took the same path and enacted the Industrial Relations Bill in the teeth of union opposition, and not without criticism from many other quarters. The first trials of strength in the Industrial Relations Court give no encouragement whatever to the hope that good industrial relations will be enforced by legislation; and already, under the threat of a totally destructive collision of interests, and within the framework of a policy to control inflation, there dawns the possibility of new conventions to govern corporate bargaining and decision – to regulate mutual expectations in a way which can still preserve a free society. If, then, the Industrial Relations Act, as it now stands, should prove unworkable or unnecessary, it will have left behind it a monument relevant to my present purpose, and indicative of the search to which I point – the Code of Industrial Relations Practice, a statement, in terms of conventions, of what good industrial behaviour should be like.

Conventions embody expectations. They also impose limitations. Social life as we know it rests on a set of tensions between the free person and the common good, with free and voluntary associations abounding in order to prevent the polarization of the individual and the state or central power. On the one side we insist that persons are ends in themselves, and must not be treated detrimentally, without consent, as means to ends outside themselves; their interests must not be subordinated to any 'totality' or totalitarian structure or myth as though they were mere parts, without a finality, an ultimate worth of their own. On the other side we aspire to a community in which all the members fulfil their own lives, create their own totality, by contributing to the common life. Hence the first demand of community is limitation – an ethics which requires the limitation of self-interest where it conflicts with the interests of other persons or of the community itself. The law properly sets minimum standards of such self-limitation which it will enforce, if necessary, with penal sanctions. But the more the law is driven to intervene in this way, the more evident it is that individuals are living below the human possibilities of their personhood – they are subjecting themselves to be governed by exaction because they will not rise to the demands of giving and concession; and the more evident it is that society is becoming less of a community and more of a totality, dominating, restricting and taking from its members because it can no longer believe in or rely on enough of their voluntary personal contribution to ensure viability. A healthy community requires that the limitation essential to corporate life be, so far as possible, inward and voluntary; the product of conscience, conviction, inward persuasion and belief, and not imposed from without. It is the realization of this, and of the dependence of conscience on a quickening religious faith, which makes the jurisprudence of Lord Devlin so attractive to a Christian theologian. He could conclude his Maccabaean Lecture with the statement that 'without the help of Christian teaching the law will fail'; he can quote

Cardinal Newman, from a letter, 'An *imperium* there always must be in the State's *imperio* so long as man retains a conscience and free will'; he can relate that conscience to the image of God in man and the dwelling in him of the Holy Ghost;[9] and he can deliver a whole lecture to the British Psycho-Analytical Society on the practical necessity of a sense of guilt in the human mind if law and order are to be maintained, sheer enforcement being simply impossible. He concluded his lecture with these words, which are echoed elsewhere in his writings:

> It is not necessary to be a Christian to say that in the western world there is not even a discernible sign of anything that is capable of replacing Christianity in the mind of the populace as the provider of the moral force vital for the maintenance of good order.[10]

Limitation there must be, and voluntary, self-limitation. But even this does not mean, and cannot be left to, individual decision, unaided, unsupported, from moment to moment. Community lives by expectation: the principle of limitation has to be written into conventions, giving implicit guidance to the individual when self-limitation is expected of him, and to the community when it may properly expect it, or assume it to be forthcoming. A fully-grown religious ethics, like that of the Judaeo-Christian tradition, goes far beyond these utilitarian considerations into the supreme worth of sacrifice, in the transcendence of self in subordination and service to the other. But even so, limitation there must be—even a limitation upon 'what love demands', or what 'compassion' may require, to turn for a moment to the language of situation ethics. Limitation must protect the agent in a good deed as well as restrain him from a bad one. Compassion, for instance, as a motive could destroy a potentially good nurse in a week, if she allowed herself to 'feel' for every patient the emotion she would feel for her own child or fiancé in a comparable situation; compassion has its place in professional care, but it must be kept strictly in its place if the care is to be effective. The 'compassion' (or scriptural legalism) which impels a gift of money to every casual beggar at the railway terminus may simply hasten alcoholics along the way to self-destruction. Limitation is also a dictate of prudence: there are actions and relationships which, though not wrong in themselves, may be, in given circumstances, dangerous, by involving persons in predictable risk; a convention of restraint in these circumstances guards against reckless exposure to fore-seeable harm. Convention, being voluntary, relational and im-plicit, can always be disregarded, of course, in obedience to particular demand; sometimes it must be. But observe the risk: if a convention has a particular protective function in relation to any of the more sensitive areas of human relationship – for example, that which confines sexual union to within marriage or that which attributes the right in a fetus normally to come to birth – every time it is broken at the dictate of a momentary or individualist demand of 'compassion' or 'love' it is weakened, and other persons are left more at risk; and conventions, once eroded by disuse, defiance or ridicule, are not always re-estab-lished (as re-established they will be, if they serve a fundamental human need) without the social disfigurement of extreme re-action. Permissiveness invites the Puritan backlash: public figures make themselves ridiculous; a generation is confused; and the sensitive suffer as the more precious elements in human encounter are distorted, caricatured and vilified in the aggres-sive debate. In recent proceedings, for instance, over a publica-tion alleged to be obscene one ingredient in the defence was that children were unlikely to be 'corrupted' because the references made to sexual intercourse would make it seem more repulsive to them than attractive. To a Christian theologian this defence is immoral to the point of blasphemy.

Conventions, it has been said, embody expectations; they im-pose limitations; they result in liberation – liberation for the individual and the conditions of freedom for the community. Assurance is itself a liberating force. Where there is a conven-tion of honesty and fair dealing, buyer and seller can negotiate together without crippling suspicion or fear: to have 'a garage you can trust' is the car-owner's dream. An accepted convention of marital fidelity and some sort of domestic solidarity enables friends and neighbours to associate freely without fear of family disruption. If, in their inter-personal behaviour, unmarried people of student age are less strictly governed by the con-ventions of an earlier generation, they develop conventions of their own, because assurance of some sort, 'knowing what to expect of one another', is necessary for security, even in the communes of protest: uncertainty, 'not knowing where you are', is the very devil when you are feeling your way into life.

As in personal behaviour, so also on the social level: it is worth reflecting how much more constricted social and economic life would be – how much less free – were not so much of it governed by an extensive conventionalized morality. A vast amount of business, including the whole banking system, is conducted on the basis of trust. There are safeguards built into it, to deter or protect from the fraudulent – to prevent the abuse of cheques, bank credit cards and the like – and these are necessary and should be stringent. But without the supposition that most people are honest most of the time, that more cheques will be honoured than dishonoured, and, indeed, that banks are trustworthy custodians of the accounts held in them, the system could not work at all. Or consider what happens in a society where it can no longer be assumed that people normally speak the truth: where no one can really believe *anything* he hears on the wireless or reads in the newspaper; where the police are so corrupt that any evidence can be falsified to secure a conviction – or an acquittal; where everyone lies in the returns made to public authorities, and no public servant or politician can be trusted not to lie if a lie suits him – no one could for a moment imagine such a society to be free. The whole of life would be enmeshed in checks and balances; and since there would be no trust anywhere, even these could not deliver from suspicion and fear. The only deliverer is a common morality: a morality personal to each member of society, in the sense that each is the moral agent whose decisions have to be relied on most of the time; and a morality embodied in institutions, especially in conventions, in order to provide for the individual what a governor or flywheel provides for an engine receiving intermittent surges of power, to maximize the creative thrust and to minimize the drag or lag. Convention is thus society's strongest preservative against both anarchy and the tyranny of an all-pervading punitive and coercive law.

But convention makes great demands, for it stems from belief. It embodies in institutional form what the community believes to be of worth – specific beliefs about the worth of people whether old or young or still unborn, whether rich or poor, clever or simple, and of whatever colour or creed; beliefs about the value of human relationships and the common interest in the truths upon which they stand. The beliefs have their history, and it can be traced in the twin roots of our culture, Greek philosophy and the Judaeo-Christian religion. It is not my purpose to trace this history in these lectures.[11] My theme now is the *artifice* of ethics, the conviction that moral insights are precious, are to be striven for, and, once attained, are to be embodied in institutions, of which the convention is of most general practical use. There are two reasons why this task is especially pressing today.

The first, and minor, reason is that a complex of circumstances has put the old conventions under strain. Conventions are strongest in a fairly stable society, where the common morality is strong and the processes both of social control and of transmission to the next generation are well established. Today these conditions prevail in diminishing areas; in some they have almost vanished. The common morality has been fragmented under the impact of major wars; of economic, political and social revolution; and of the challenge of new knowledge to established patterns of belief, conveyed with hitherto unknown intensity and immediacy through wireless and television. Social control is weakened by mobility, and by the penetration of radio into even the most closely guarded of homes and parochial or other cultural enclosures. The processes of transmission, that is, of moral education, have themselves been extensively dismantled, partly by deliberate policies with doctrinaire foundations, partly for lack of a language or other symbols – hitherto provided by religion – both strong and acceptable enough to be a carrier of a moral tradition and its interpreter to a new society. We are now, therefore, a generation in search of new conventions by which to live.

This fact provides the second impulse to urgency. The very knowledge which has disrupted the old certainties has created new sciences, new technologies, new instruments with which human society can be manipulated, improved or destroyed. New military technology calls for a new politics, new political morality. New medical technology calls for a new professional ethics – new decisions on questions never raised before, options never open before. New electronic technology calls for a new ethics of mass communication, even of the exploration of outer space. New industrial capacities, the new threat of the exhaustion of fossil fuels, the new imbalance between population growth and natural resources, all these together present the new combined menace of pollution, saturation and exhaustion of the earth by which we live – all calling for a new ethics of the use of productive and reproductive powers. The old moralities, in their old articulation, will not serve to meet these needs. We have to create a new morality for them, extracting wisdom from the old, but expecting to find new demands for which that wisdom did not provide, and so to meet them by moral craftsmanship of a high order. This I have called the artifice of ethics; and this, a ranging to and fro between the old and the new, is a lecture theme of which Bishop Moorhouse would not, I hope, disapprove.

NOTES

1. Patrick Devlin, *The Enforcement of Morals*, Oxford University Press 1965, pp. 23, 25.

2. Dorothy Emmet, *Rules, Roles and Relations*, Macmillan 1966.

3. R. S. Downie and Elizabeth Telfer, *Respect for Persons*, Allen and Unwin 1969.

4. R. S. Downie, *Roles and Values*, Methuen 1971. Cf. D. K. Lewis, *Conventions: A Philosophic Study*, Harvard University Press 1969.

5. Sydney Bailey, *Prohibitions and Restraints in War*, Oxford University Press 1972.

6. H. L. A. Hart, *Law, Liberty and Morality*, Oxford University Press 1963.

7. See Paul Ramsey, *Deeds and Rules in Christian Ethics*, Oliver and Boyd 1965, enlarged ed., Scribners, New York 1967, for a forceful intervention in the debate.

8. D. Emmet, op. cit., p. 41. Helen Oppenheimer has recently carried the philosophical debate further in 'Ought and Is', *Theology* LXXVI, Feb. 1973, p. 59.

9. Devlin, op. cit., pp. 25, 119, 100.

10. *The Times*, 10 Nov. 1964. It was not his purpose to consider the moral worth of other religious traditions in other cultures.

11. I attempted a summary of it once before, in *Not Yet the Epitaph*, University of Exeter 1968.

2

Insight and Institution:
1. In the Bible

It was not altogether by accident that the first of these lectures
developed a theme which is not to be heard enthusiastically on
everybody's lips today, or read in every journal. It may be, of
course, that the theme is too trivial to discuss: that moral insights require institutional embodiment and, in particular, create
conventions, is so obvious that the working moralist has no need
to labour it. But there may be another reason. We tend to put
out of mind what we do not like; and such a theme will find few
takers at a time of general hostility to 'structures', 'institutions'
and 'establishments' of every kind – particularly to 'conventional
morality'. To be contemporary is to appeal to some higher source
or standard by which to judge them; then to let utopianism take
over, in the belief that if we could only 'change the structures'
the barriers between our goals and our attainment would dis-
appear. We are not the first to do this: Christians have again
and again appealed to scripture, to the pure word of Jesus, by
which to judge the evil and the inadequacy of their dying world.
And they were right to do so: that is precisely what the word of
Jesus is for, to judge *every* word and work of man, and then to
offer a re-creative grace to give new life. And the dying world
has been quickened by this means, again and again: this is the
tideway of Christian history. But observe two things. First, that
in the quickening a new institution of some sort is created to
embody the new insight, to preserve and extend it, to make it
run and set men running with it. Secondly, that this process, far
from stultifying the appeal to scripture, is entrenched in scripture; neither the Old Testament nor the New makes sense without it. To sketch the relation of insight to institution in scripture
is the intention of this lecture.

We may begin with a paradox. It is reasonable to suppose in a Christian community that morality is somehow founded on, or at least bound up with, the teaching of Jesus Christ. Yet when we examine that teaching we do not find in it the fundamentals of a moral law: nowhere does Jesus lay down those basic requirements of social existence – of a moral community – found in all codes of morality, such as respect for parents, and the prohibitions of murder, theft, false evidence and adultery. He takes all these for granted; they were already part of the law entrenched in Israel's life; his purpose was to point back to their true meaning, to bring all evasions of their absolute demand under judgment.[1] It is St Paul who has to lay down the law in this sense, to teach the fundamentals of social obligation and protection, precisely because in his Gentile mission he had no moral community behind him: he had to create one out of the mixed gathering of Gentile converts whom he brought together into his churches, men and women of all conditions, bond and free, with no other common factor than their being found together in the cosmopolitan cities of the Graeco-Roman empire. Jews of the Dispersion, when they joined his churches, gave them a nucleus of people accustomed to living, so far as they could, by the Jewish law. Their existence brought its own problems, as is evident from the earlier epistles, especially Galatians and Romans. But it is evident from the long lists of wrongs prohibited and virtues commended, and from St Paul's replies to questions put to him by the Corinthian church,[2] that his first task was to create moral conventions in his infant churches in order to give them elementary moral cohesion and stability. He called this task feeding them with milk, fit for babes: the full meat of the gospel was too strong for them until they had become morally adult.[3] He had to lay a moral foundation on which the Christian structure could be built. Jesus, in his ministry within the Jewish community, could take such a foundation for granted.

But how was this foundation laid among the Jews? The common phrase, 'the law and the prophets', and the arrangement of the Old Testament which puts the Pentateuch, the books of the law, first, and the histories and the prophets later, may well obscure a very elementary truth, that institution follows insight, that the law developed, not apart from the prophets, but in response to their work.

The subject is, of course, technical, and one which Old Testament scholars have unravelled at length.[4] There is no book of Hebrew ethics in the Bible; we have to search out the ethics from the whole literature which was a product of the community's life. And the search is not confined to the Pentateuch, the books of the law; nor to the prophets, as to a separate or independent source. Indeed, the vertical division between books has to be very largely abandoned if the development of a moral community is to be understood as an historical process, and if that development is to be related to the Hebrew response to God. As every student in the critical tradition knows, the horizontal lines of division are far more significant, those evidences of re-writing which run through the Pentateuch and the histories alike, and which are known, in the most elementary analysis, as the Jahwistic, Elohistic, Deuteronomic and Priestly traditions respectively. These revisions are to be related to the activity of the prophets: they embody a theology, an understanding of God, which develops and deepens; they embody moral demands, which develop and deepen in response to the more demanding knowledge of God; they embody institutions, some to register, as it were, the moral insight and the moral demand, some to commend and support it, some to relate it back to its source, in God.

The law is one such institution; and although the seventh of the Thirty-Nine Articles of Religion, following Reformation practice, divides the law into three sorts, that 'touching Ceremonies and Rites' which we call the cultus, 'the Civil precepts', and 'the Commandments which are called Moral', we may make no such division in our study of ethics. Each of these gave institutional expression to an ethical insight and demand, related to the corporate and personal life of the Hebrew people in which civil and religious duties were one whole moral obligation. The priestly cultus was a profoundly ethical institution: it celebrated the holy and righteous nature of God, and the nature and demands of his covenant with Israel; it set forth the sovereignty of Israel's King, the worship and loyalty due to him for what he was, the thanksgiving for what he had done, the obedience which he could command; it reckoned realistically with sin as an

offence to God and an infection in the nature of men, both re-
quiring, in relevant senses of the word, to be purged away.

The histories, too, are a moral institution. Each time the
history of Israel and Judah was re-written, a new doctrine of God
and his dealings with his people was written into it. In particular there was the doctrine of God's judgment shown in the working of history which comes as a refrain in the narratives of the
kings:

> Now it came to pass ... that Hezekiah the son of Ahaz king of Judah
> began to reign. ... And he did that which was right in the eyes of the
> LORD: ... he removed the high places, and brake the pillars; ... he
> trusted in the LORD, the God of Israel; ... he clave to the LORD, he
> departed not from following his commandments. ... And the LORD
> was with him; whithersoever he went forth he prospered ... (II Kings
> 18.1ff.)

> Amon was twenty and two years old when he began to reign; and he
> reigned two years in Jerusalem. ... And he did that which was evil in
> the sight of the LORD; ... and he forsook the LORD the God of his
> fathers. ... And the servants of Amon conspired against him, and put
> the king to death in his own house. (II Kings 21.19ff.)

> Jehoahaz was twenty and three years old when he began to reign; and
> he reigned three months in Jerusalem; ... and he did that which was
> evil in the sight of the LORD. ... And Pharaoh-necoh put him in bands
> at Riblah in the land of Hamath, that he might not reign in Jerusalem,
> and put the land to a tribute ... (II Kings 23.31ff.)

To teach history in this way is to teach a moral view of the world
– whether it is an *adequate* view is another question, not discussed here. It was a view wrought by the prophets out of their
wrestling on the one side with their awareness of God and on the
other with the facts of the history of his people, with its terrible
climax in the destruction of Jerusalem followed by the Exile in
the times of Jeremiah and Ezekiel, and with its restoration at the
time of the Second Isaiah. History, so understood and so written,
is a moral institution.

So were the Holy Writings, the Hagiographa, the Psalms, Job
and the Wisdom literature. They reflect, in their different
literary forms, the whole way of life developed within the law,
the covenant. In them we see the Jew, the devout Jew, the
ordinary Jew, learning to walk with God; learning to keep the
covenant; bearing the yoke of the kingdom; celebrating the

Name of the King; pursuing holiness; atoning for unholiness; looking for a future which would come with the coming of his King. Even the myths in which he dreamt about his paradisal origin are outstanding from their kind precisely because of the morality written into them. 'And God saw that it was good'; this simple refrain, written almost liturgically into the creation narrative, separated the Hebrew people, and all Hebrew ethics, from the dualism of other cultures; it preserved them, and us, from the notion that matter is essentially evil – 'God saw everything that he had made, and, behold, it was very good', including man and woman, naked and not ashamed. Here is the ground of a whole morality written into the language of myth: a morality of still unrealized importance for man's relation to the material world, his scientific exploration of it and technical manipulation of its sources, including his own biological resources. It came from the insight of men whom we call prophets, those who saw that the Lord of history was also the Lord of nature and its creator; and who saw in marriage, a man cleaving to his wife, an apt symbol of the covenant, of God cleaving to his people, and suffering with them as their history comes painfully under judgment. Such a myth is a moral institution.

There emerges, therefore, from this survey of the literature of the Old Testament, one pattern or paradigm by which Hebrew ethics may be studied, and perhaps taught; it subordinates ethics to religious insight, as it treats the institutions which were the carriers of the common morality as secondary to the religious and moral discernment of the great historic figures, Moses and the prophets; and it rests on a concept of the unity of the diverse literature of the Old Testament which I hope critical study will allow. It presupposes, of course, a theological treatment of the Old Testament – a theology written into it already, not one read into it – recognizing that such a treatment cannot dispense with historical and archaeological analyses but is rather enriched by them. It is a valid historical study, for instance, to establish which ingredients for the Pentateuch have their roots or parallels in other ancient Middle Eastern codes, that of Hammurabi, for instance, or the Sumerian codes. It is a theological question to ask what is meant when the authority of Israel's God – 'Thus saith the Lord', or 'The Lord spake unto Moses and said' – is claimed for them. The question can be answered only when asked in the context of Israel's theological understanding of its own history; and this the prophets gave it.

In the theological tradition the pivot on which all Israel's history turns is the Exodus and the making of the covenant on Sinai. Here the common political notion of a contract or treaty between peoples began its development into a religious symbol, embodying God's initiative met by Israel's response, with the pledge of mutual loyalty sealed in sacrifice. The terms of the compact are set out in the Book of the Covenant, in Exodus 21-23. Here already elements of the common code of social behaviour – the 'natural necessities' of social life, to use Professor Hart's phrase[5] – are brought under the sanctions of religion, and extended. Human life and human relationships are of more worth than property rights; even the life of a beast, an extension of the life of man its owner, has a claim high enough to override human enmity.[6] Here is a code, an instrument of what was to become law, embodying moral insight. Together with it went a teaching instrument, making the precepts memorable – the Ten Commandments or Decalogue, itself worked over in different recensions as new insights had to be given expression.[7]

With the covenant stood the principle of obedience, the absolute obedience owed to a king in that culture, and now extended to infinity in God the King. The prophets, pronouncing 'the word of the Lord', recalled earthly kings and people to that obedience when they strayed from it. They extended the terms of that obedience as the change of historical context demanded it – the change, for instance, from the nomadic life to the settled life in Canaan; or from the period of imperial expansion to contraction to the point of siege, to the going into exile in Babylon. They deepened the terms of obedience also, by internalizing the keeping of the law: in the name of the God of 'loving-kindnesses' they required this of men, this as the motive of good action among men – deeper than mere obedience to a law, deeper than the merely utilitarian avoidance of retribution, with which the 'judgment' theory of history threatened them. Amos, in the opening of his book, extended the judgment of the God of Israel over neighbouring peoples in the oracles of doom which he pronounced against them for their unnatural cruelty and the like, over neighbours who did not acknowledge this God's sovereignty over them. Hosea, in his use of the symbolism of courtship and marriage to illuminate the covenant – a theme henceforth of profound importance, swelling out of the Old Testament into the New – brought the truths of forgiveness and restoration in alongside of faithfulness as ingredients in the covenant. This, and more like it, I have called the searching out and proclamation of moral insight: it needed institutions yet to embody it.

These were provided in several ways by the Deuteronomic reform: another re-writing of history, administrative reforms like the centralizing of the cultus in Jerusalem, and above all a new recension of the law.[8] The new law was put in narrative form and written into the story of Moses and the Exodus; it was thus built into the covenant, and made the embodiment of the response of Israel to its Saviour-God. God is seen, whether in chastening or in favour, as a God of love and faithfulness; these must therefore become the prime motives of obedience.[9] The law becomes a means of identification, even of communication, with God: it is to be bound upon the brow, and on the doorposts of the house, in place of the tattoos and threshold gods of Israel's neighbours. Alongside of the corporate solidarity of the nation within the covenant Deuteronomy sets the complementary principle of personal liability, a principle developed by Ezekiel and Jeremiah, in the figure of the sour grapes, even in apparent contradiction to one of the extensions of the second Mosaic commandment.[10] To read the Deuteronomic law is to feel oneself living with a closely-knit, brotherly, godly and civilized society, however far the vision was from the reality into which broke, all too soon, the destruction of Jerusalem and the Babylonian captivity.

The prophets of the exile and the return, Jeremiah, Ezekiel and the Second Isaiah, together gave Judah a new concept of holiness and a new theology of redemptive suffering. Holiness became no longer the distance, the separateness, of majesty, infinitely magnified, but an ethical purity so wounded by sin and injustice that it cannot hold itself back from action to remove it. That action could be with power, with a high hand, with war in history, and with the sword. It could be also in suffering, when God himself and the people in covenant with him take the suffering into themselves, and so turn it from others. The fulfilment of the Suffering Servant, of Israel identified in suffering with its Saviour-God, lies beyond the Old Testament and in the New. But the contemplation of the holiness of God became a new motive in Hebrew ethics, summed up in the command of Leviticus 19.2, 'Ye shall be holy: for I the LORD your God am holy.'

This insight too created its own institutional embodiments in the Code of Holiness, in Leviticus 17-26, setting out the insepar-able twin requirements of God – ethical holiness of life, personal and corporate, and the sacrifices of expiation for sins committed as well as of thanksgiving and praise. We err if we set prophet against priest in the Old Testament: the priest embodied, in ritual act, what the prophet taught. That his task was dangerous is not denied; that the priestly cultus could be exploited without adequate ethical demand or response was and remains a fact of life, men being as they are. But an understanding of Hebrew religion and ethics requires that the integral relation of prophet to priest, of insight to institution, be discerned.

The fruit of this, at its best, was good and godly living, men learning to 'walk with God' (*halakah*) by interpreting the law in terms of loving by commandment. Jesus, in giving his summary of all the law and the prophets, linked together the command to love God with all the heart, recited daily in the *Shema*, with the command to love the neighbour as oneself, the one from Deuter-onomy, the other from Leviticus.[11] The delight of the devout Jew in this pursuit, in the fulfilling of the law, is written large in the Psalms, especially 19 and 119; it shews itself in actual lives, not least in those of Zacharias and Elizabeth, Mary and Joseph, Simeon and Anna, with which the New Testament opens.

The New Testament, in one respect, stands in sharp contrast to the Old. The Old Testament shews the development of the in-stitution of Israel, spread over many centuries, in response to the insights of numbers of men. The New Testament records the response to one man, Jesus of Nazareth, and the institutional embodiment of that response, in well under one hundred years of the church's life. It is common ground among teachers now that the first response to Jesus was what we may, in this context, call theological: when men analysed within themselves the re-lated experiences, of being with Jesus in his ministry, of receiving the Pentecostal Spirit after his resurrection, and of sharing in the Spirit-filled community when acceptance of the *kerygma*, the story preached, led on to baptism, then they were driven to express their understanding of Jesus in the theological language which they inherited from the Old Testament. The second response was ethical: whenever the action of God in Christ was preached, the teaching of the way of life required followed upon it. The third response was institutional: long before the canon of the New Testament was closed, while even the earlier epistles were being written and the gospel traditions were still being formed, the church had created institutions to embody, protect and perpetuate its first impulsive ethical responses: to provide, in fact, for the moral life of the community. In St Paul's earliest surviving epistle, the first to the Thessalonians, he reveals himself as a Christian scribe, teaching a Christian *halakah* – 'how they ought to walk and to please God'.[12]

Household codes, a common teaching instrument of the time, were adapted for use in the household churches of the new Christian communities: the code of mutual subordination, derived from the Servant Christ's submission to death at the hands of men, was developed into particular duties for the identifiable groups in the church – husbands, wives, parents, children, masters, slaves. It appears discernibly in Colossians, fully developed in Ephesians, and woven, probably, into a baptismal homily in I Peter, all evidence of general use.[13]

Deeds, it may be thought, afford more eloquent proof than words. And deeds there were: the early church very soon institutionalized its charity. The first attempt at a community of goods, a primitive Christian communism, ended in disaster, in the episode of Ananias and Sapphira.[14] The apostles ought to have known better: disordered human nature is not perfected overnight, and Christian moral institutions have to guard against residual self-interest and cupidity as much as to provide for personal and corporate generosity. So charity was newly organized on different bases: the daily distribution, resulting in the ordaining of the Seven for oversight – but not immune from the querulousness of the Grecian widows;[15] the working out of rough-and-ready distinctions between the deserving and the undeserving poor – to protect the community against the work-shy in Thessalonica, exploiting the common expectation of the End very soon, and to free the community from obligation towards more tiresome widows in the church addressed in I Timothy.[16] The wholesome realism of these records is of the utmost importance to us when we come to consider the sort of authority which attaches to such unambiguous precepts of Jesus as 'Give to him that asketh thee, and from him that would borrow of thee turn not away'.[17] It underlies the distinction between first-order principles and second-order rules which we shall meet again in this exposition.

The same lesson stands clear in the record of the major charitable effort in the New Testament, St Paul's collection among his Gentile churches for the relief of the famine-stricken church of Judaea. This was more, in conception, than an act of organized compassion, like a first-century OXFAM; it was also, in St Paul's treatment of it, a theological gesture, a demonstration of the new unity of Jew and Gentile in the common life of the church; one word used for the Gentile contribution was *koinonia*, the word used also for the fellowship of the apostolic church in Acts, and for the fellowship of the Spirit in St Paul's trinitarian formula at the end of II Corinthians.[18] It gave St Paul an enormous amount of trouble – the inevitable imputation of bad motives and the like, and some challenge to his authority – against which he had to guard by letters to accredited persons; but it resulted in an entrenched Christian institution, the Sunday collection – the offering in the weekly gathering in fellowship and communion – derived from St Paul's own brilliant insight into what the new unity of Jew and Gentile demanded in the face of one historical event, a famine.

These are examples of the provision which the primitive church was driven to make both to carry out a good purpose in obedience to what it had learned of the love of God in Christ, and to protect itself from sin, disorder, ill-consequence, in so doing. It would be tedious to search out every possible example of the same process at work. Two others may be given, however, to illustrate an abiding duty in the church, to devise rules of a sort which will embody in its life its obedience to some principles laid upon it by Christ, and which will continue to witness to that principle even when the position regulated is disordered to the point of frustrating the principle itself. First, St Matthew's gospel records two sayings of Jesus which, if taken as literal command-

ments, would exclude his disciples from established judicial processes: the one is 'Swear not at all', and the other, 'If any man
would go to law with thee, and take away thy coat, let him have
thy cloke also.' Later the same evangelist puts into the mouth of
Jesus a procedure for the settlement of disputes, involving, after
personal reconciliation has failed, first a hearing before two or
three witnesses, then a hearing before the church, with expulsion
or excommunication as the penalty for rejecting its decision.[19]
St Paul, while forbidding his Corinthians to go to law with one
another before 'unbelievers', clearly operates a system of judicial
hearing and excommunication against a serious offender; and he
himself was arrested on his last visit to Jerusalem while in the
temple fulfilling a vow made in Cenchreae.[20] Clearly, the sayings of Jesus assert, in epigrammatic form, the first principles of
always telling the simple truth, and of generosity both in submission to the point of material loss and in ready forgiveness.
But the church, in its second-order rules, as attested by St
Matthew and St Paul, had to witness as best it could to the first-
order principle, while providing regulations for defective situations.

The same process is embodied in my second example, in which
a first-order principle about marriage is asserted by Jesus, not
only in his declaring any marriage after divorce to be adulter-
ous, but also in his absolutely forbidding 'putting asunder', the
separation of husband and wife, whether re-marriage followed
or not.[21] This principle is entirely consistent with the covenant
theology for which the marriage covenant provided a symbolism
from Hosea in the Old Testament to the end of Revelation in
the New.[22] From its grounding by Christ in an appeal to that
which was 'from the beginning', the word in Genesis 2.24 about
a man cleaving to his wife and their becoming one flesh, it was
seen to represent the primordial will of God expressed in the
very act of creation. No principle could seem to be more un-
assailable. Yet assailed it was, not by the church, but by men
in the hardness of their hearts; and the church, driven to
regulate in some way the defective situations arising from this,
had to devise second-order rules which, while they witness
obliquely to the first-order principle already broken, clearly de-
part legislatively from it. This is seen in the so-called Matthaean
exception, *mē epi porneia*, or *parektos logou porneias*. It is seen

also in St Paul's prescription for the Christian spouse whose
heathen partner leaves him, the so-called Pauline privilege.[23]
The 'privilege' was, in fact, only one element in the complex of
institutional rules, exemplified in I Corinthians 7, as in the beginning of Romans 7, by which the church began to protect its
insight into the essential mutuality of marriage. St Matthew
appears to have written the rules of his church – the source of
his tradition – into the words of Jesus; St Paul clearly distinguished his rules from the saying of Jesus : 'to the rest say I,'
he wrote, 'not the Lord'; but the reality was the same to both.
The church was doing its duty, working out, by moral reasoning, rules appropriate both to the principle and to the ruptured
situation. The church has done this ever since; it remains its
duty to this day. And perennial confusion is caused by a failure
to distinguish between the first-order principle and the second-
order rule. The absoluteness inherent in the first must not be
attributed to the second; and the contingency imposed by
circumstance on the second must not be allowed to dilute the
first.

What then is the worth, the function, of the words of Jesus?
They are not the words of law. They stand eternally in judgment over all law, all convention, all institutions, all human
action, all human aspiration. They shew up the gulf between
the humanly attainable and the true. They drive man out of his
comfortable refuges to hear, as Elijah heard, standing before the
mouth of his cave, the voice of the sovereign will of God, pro-
claiming the way of the kingdom where all life is an obedient
response in love to love. Then, from discontent, they draw him
on to deeper insight within the given grace; and so to new institutions to live in, until he should be drawn out and on again,
moving still in the half-light of dawn until the day breaks which
is at hand.[24]

NOTES

1. Cf. e.g. Matt. 5.17-48; Mark 7.5-13.
2. See e.g. I Cor. 6.9-10; 7; Gal. 5.6-14; Eph. 4.17-6.24; Col. 3.5-11,
12-17.
3. I Cor. 3.2
4. See e.g. Anthony Phillips, *Ancient Israel's Criminal Law: A New
Approach to the Decalogue*, Basil Blackwell 1970.

5. H. L. A. Hart, *The Concept of Law*, Oxford University Press 1961.
6. Ex. 22.5.
7. Ex. 20.1-17; 34.10-26; Deut. 5.7-21; 27.15-26.
8. See especially Deut. 12-21.
9. Deut. 8.5; 10.12-26.
10. Deut. 24.16; Ezek. 18; Jer. 31.29f.
11. Matt. 22.37-40; Deut. 6.4-9; Lev. 19.18.
12. I Thess. 4.1.
13. Col. 3.18-4.1; Eph. 5.21-6.10; I Peter 2.13-3.12.
14. Acts 4.32-5.11.
15. Acts 6.1-6.
16. I Thess. 5.14; II Thess. 3.6-15; I Tim. 5.1-16.
17. Matt. 5.42.
18. Acts 2.42; Rom. 15.26; II Cor. 8.4; 9.13; 13.13.
19. Matt. 5.34, 40; 18.15-18.
20. I Cor. 6.1-8; 5.1-5; Acts 18.18; 21.23.
21. Mark 10.2-12; Luke 16.18.
22. E.g., Hos. 1-3; Jer. 31.32; Eph. 5.23-33; Rev. 19.7 9
23. Matt. 19.9; 5.32; I Cor. 7.12-17.
24. Rom. 13.12f.

3

Insight and Institution:
2. In a Church

My purpose in this lecture is to trace how a church formulates and commends its moral judgments. I bring to it some generalizations drawn from the narrow range of my own historical interests, and some experience of participation in the processes which I describe in recent years. It is not, I hope, mere insularity which inclines me to begin from where I am, from within the Church of England rather than from something wider called 'the Anglican Communion', or from something wider still, the church universal, whatever that is. My subject is a moral tradition; and whereas other churches than the English within the Anglican Communion vigorously formulate moral judgments, as in their autonomy they are entitled to, they too work from within a tradition; and that tradition stemmed from England, from its canon law certainly, and, in some places, from its common law also. I take as my point of departure the century before the Reformation, when the Church of England was fully integrated with the canonical jurisdiction of the Church of Rome on the one side, and with the juridical reality of the realm of England, a sovereign state, on the other. There and then our moral tradition was visibly one branch of the vine of the whole Western church, stemming from a common theological and moral root. Since, therefore, we have now diverged, and since today we are minded to explore the extent of our divergence, there may be value in our beginning just before the divergence began.

I

The moral tradition of a church may be considered in at least three aspects. In one it is seen as the norms of life and conduct taught to its members *pro salute animae*, for the good of their souls, and accepted by them, as persons, at moments of liturgical commitment, like baptism and confirmation: so *normam vivendi docere* is, and has always been, part of the ministerial task. In this aspect, moral theology merges with other theological pursuits – spiritual theology, ascetic theology, sacramental theology, and all that concerns the life of grace and the search for the vision of God. In another aspect the moral tradition is seen as standards or canons governing the corporate life of the community, the church: that which is believed to manifest its theological character as the Body of Christ and to provide for its inner cohesion as a body, as a human society. Both of these aspects fall together within the ambit of canon law – a science which has, throughout the centuries, tended to become autonomous in isolation from the other theological disciplines at its peril, and to the hurt of the whole church. The third aspect of the moral tradition of a church is the part it plays in establishing norms for that particular political society in which it is set – or in challenging those set by the secular society for itself. Each of these three aspects is represented in the Anglican moral tradition, and though I cannot hope, because of my personal limitations, to keep a balance between all three of them, I hope none will be totally neglected.

In Pre-Reformation England the moral guidance of the faithful and the moral cohesion of the church were both taken care of in the normal pastoral ministry of word and sacraments, and in the exercise of the discipline of the canon law. English parish priests were bidden, by provincial and diocesan synodal constitutions, to instruct their people, in the English tongue, out of the Creed, the Lord's Prayer, the Ten Commandments, the seven sacraments and the seven deadly sins.[1] The virtues, and the hope of Heaven, were taught out of *exempla*, the lives of the Saints – though perhaps some of these should be written as 'lives'.[2] The vices, all actions *contra bonos mores et decorum*, were treated in the canon law as *crimina et excessus*, and punishment ('penance', *pena*) was prescribed for them in the canon law and meted out in the sentences of the ecclesiastical courts. Failure to submit to penance – i.e. to undergo the humiliation of the penitential procession, or the public *fustigatio* (a whipping, not a flogging), or to pay the bursal penance, the fine, would incur excommunication. A clergyman, still remaining obdurate, could be incarcerated in the bishop's prison – but not a layman. The 'custom of the realm', by which was meant the king's judges, would not allow the church to imprison laymen, though it might impose its other corporal or bursal penances upon them. Against the obdurate layman, however, the bishop had a remedy: after forty days he could write to the king for the caption of the excommunicate; a royal writ could then order the arrest of the offender, *'ut quos timor Dei a malo non revocat saltem coherceat animadversio regie potestatis'*[3] – 'that punishment at the hand of the royal power may at least restrain those whom the fear of God does not recall from evil'. Lists of the 'crimes and excesses' for which this procedure might be invoked vary in content. In addition to the strictly ecclesiastical offences, like refusal of tithes or violation of the rights and liberties of the church (poaching in the bishop's park would be an offence within these terms), William Lyndwode, the great English canonist of the fifteenth century, lists perjury, irregularities concerning wills; fornication, adultery, incest, unnatural vice, bestiality, sacrilege, usury, simony, heresy; consulting of magicians, astrologers, soothsayers, mediums and the like; drunkenness, idolatry, and violence against certain protected classes of persons.[4]

In other words the canonical jurisdiction of the church was employed, on what in modern terms would be called an agency basis, for the enforcement of morals throughout and on behalf of the realm. There were constant tensions between the two jurisdictions and astute lawyers could play off one against the other to the advantage of a powerful client. But this accommodation between the church and the realm, established in the Middle Ages, goes some way to explain the moral tradition of the Church of England not only in the third aspect to which I alluded – the establishing of norms for the political society – but also, to some extent, in the other two. In no spirit of levity, but in full awareness of both the strengths and the weaknesses in what is implied, I would observe that the Englishman finds it difficult, until he is provoked, to distinguish between Christian behaviour and ordinary, decent, English behaviour; between what is wrong in itself and what is an offence or at least actionable at law; so far have these centuries of tradition – of which he is most probably unaware – moulded the conventions of his society and its assumptions about behaviour.

The Reformation did not significantly alter the internal structure of the system. Appeals to Rome were cut off, and the dual jurisdiction of pope and king was reduced to one single jurisdiction within one sovereign realm, that of the king, 'over all persons in all causes, as well Ecclesiastical as Temporal', supreme. (This was a turning back on itself of good medieval canonical doctrine, of the state as an exclusively Christian commonwealth, which could have, as in nature, only one head: 'for since we were one body in Christ, we should be as a monster if we had two heads'; only for Hostiensis, that head was the pope; for the princes of the Reformation it was the prince.)[5] The old canon law became the king's ecclesiastical law; actions and offences cognizable in the old ecclesiastical courts remained there, and the enforcement, or non-enforcement, of morals continued as before. Protestant Puritanism was no less punitive than Catholic puritanism; it was less tolerable, as it was self-destructive, in the long run because it repudiated the Catholic appeal to reason and tradition and purported to take all its norms direct from the letter of scripture. In my interim view, the overthrow of Puritanism with that of the Cromwellian parliamentary and military dictatorship did far more than the Reformation of a century earlier to cause the ecclesiastical jurisdiction over morals to wither away.

Wither it did – it was not formally abolished. Some old 'spiritual' offences – that is, those tried in the spiritual courts – were elevated, by sporadic acts of Parliamentary law-making, into statutory crimes: sodomy, for instance in 1533; abortion in 1803; male homosexual practices in 1861. Others, like slander, fornication and adultery, have remained in an intermediate category, known variously to common lawyers as 'liberties', 'immoral liberties' or 'unlawful acts' – mere liberties which the law will not punish as crimes (unless some other criminal ingredient is compounded, e.g., threat with slander, constituting blackmail, or force or non-age with the sexual offences); neither will it protect, favour or advance them in any way.

This tradition helped to determine the way in which the Church of England was to participate in recent reforms of the criminal law. Through one of the Councils of the Church Assembly, its Moral Welfare Council, it submitted in evidence to a Government Departmental Committee that homosexual offences between consenting adults should cease to be criminal, i.e. punishable at law, and maintained that position until in 1968 the crime was abolished.[6] On suicide it took an initiative through a small committee appointed by the then Archbishop of Canterbury (Dr G. F. Fisher); this argued, in a published report,[7] that suicide ought not to remain a crime; the government found the advice acceptable, and by the Suicide Act of 1960 the crime was abolished. Following publicity given to artificial insemination by donor in the late nineteen-fifties there was pressure to make this practice into a crime, and a Departmental Committee was set up to examine it. A small committee, appointed by the then Archbishop of Canterbury (Dr Fisher) to give evidence on behalf of the Church of England, submitted that the practice be *not* made criminal, but declared to be a mere liberty, in the sense described above. The Archbishop disagreed: he thought it ought to be criminal, and he said so in a personal submission of his own. Both submissions were published in one pamphlet, as two contributions to a Christian judgment.[8] The Departmental Committee accepted the submission of the small group, and not that of the Archbishop, and no legislation followed. (Undoubtedly, thirteen years later, the whole matter has to be examined again.)[9]

The reform of the law of divorce has a longer history, but one equally embedded in the medieval system of a divided jurisdiction. Matrimonial causes remained in the church courts until as late as 1857. The only reliefs which they could grant were those allowed by the old canon law, re-enacted in the canons of 1604: decrees of nullity, upon proof that no lawful marriage had in fact been made; and orders for separation *a mensa et thoro*, upon proof of the commission by the respondent spouse of matrimonial offences of such gravity as to endanger the moral, spiritual or physical well-being of the petitioner. Another marriage was forbidden to both parties so separated during the

lifetime of the other partner. The only escape from this jurisdiction was by way of a private Act of Parliament, entitling a
particular petitioner to marry again after a separation in the
Ecclesiastical Courts. In fact such a resort was open only to
persons of wealth and power, and only 317 such Acts were
passed between 1697 and 1850. In 1857, however, the first Matrimonial Causes Act transferred the divorce jurisdiction from the
Ecclesiastical Courts to a new Division of the High Court, and
the old canonical grounds for separation became statutory
grounds for divorce, with liberty to marry again. Once granted,
the internal logic of divorce unfolded itself, and Parliament
was under constant pressure to extend the grounds, to add to the
'matrimonial offences' on proof of which divorce could be ob-
tained. The church steadily opposed all such extension, and
generally lost: it was fighting a rearguard action, and mean-
while the substance and practice of the divorce law became less
and less morally defensible. Insanity, and cruelty with no intention to be cruel – even involuntary cruelty admitted to arise
from mental illness – were among the 'matrimonial offences',
and the notion of a relief granted to the 'innocent' against the
'guilty' all too often bore no relation to the facts.

Accordingly, in 1963, on the last occasion of conflict, the
Archbishop of Canterbury undertook to set up a committee of
his own to examine the question. This he did; and in 1966 a
committee under the Bishop of Exeter (Dr R. C. Mortimer) produced a Report, *Putting Asunder: A Divorce Law for Contemporary Society* (SPCK), which proposed that the matrimonial
offence as the ground of divorce be totally abolished, and a new
ground, the irretrievable breakdown of marriage, be substituted
for it. This, with other points of substance in the Report, was
the subject of debate in Parliament and of discussion with the
Law Commission;[10] and certainly it contributed materially to
the enactment of the Divorce Reform Act 1969, which has substituted irretrievable breakdown for the matrimonial offence as
the ground for divorce. The implications of this for the church
itself, its discipline and the guidance which it gives to its members, remained to be worked out.[11] But the church felt bound
to engage itself with the question, precisely because of its historical involvement: it shared some responsibility for the existing state of the law; it felt itself morally bound to assure, so

far as it could, that any divorce law which the state must have should be as just and effective as possible, and should do the least harm both to the first principles and institution of marriage and to the institution of law itself.

In the prolonged Parliamentary conflict which resulted in the Abortion Act, 1967, the church took what at one time looked like an influential part, but emerged in what must now be called defeat. Through another of its study groups it produced *Abortion: An Ethical Discussion.*[12] This Report, after a careful review of the moral tradition and of the indications advanced for abortion, admitted the liceity of the termination of a pregnancy which seriously threatened the 'health or well-being' of the mother – a term used to denote psychological as well as physical health in a category already made part of the case-law of the Courts but never tested on appeal. It insisted that indications like conception as a result of rape or criminal assault, or the risk of fetal deformity, be not accepted as grounds for termination in themselves, but considered circumstantially as factors affecting the health of the mother, the diagnosis and prognosis of which should be the one factor determining medical decision. In the event, the new statute admitted indications external to the mother, including social indications extending to an estimated adverse effect on other children of her family, as grounds for termination in themselves. There is at present widespread disquiet at the number and distribution of abortions effected under the terms of the Act.

In the current debates on 'euthanasia', and on the reform of the law relating to tissue-transplantation, churchmen are taking a significant part. They have acted also, both individually and in relevant Boards and Councils, official, voluntary and ecumenical, to influence Government administrative action in relation to economic aid for developing countries, the improvement of race relations, industrial relations, housing policies, nuclear warfare, gambling and the like.

To this summary recital of action taken to influence legislation or governmental policies may be added a history of formal action to influence personal decision in an area not governed by the law, namely the practice of contraception. In this matter the Church of England has made no independent statements, but has involved itself closely in formulating resolutions of successive Lambeth Conferences, from 1908 to 1958.[13] The Conference of 1908 condemned the practice of contraception as 'demoralizing to character and hostile to national welfare', and commended doctors who would have nothing to do with it. In that of 1920 its extension was alleged to 'threaten the race'; and 'the teaching which, under the name of science and religion, encourages married people in the deliberate cultivation of sexual union as an end in itself' was, in Resolution 68, steadfastly opposed. In 1930, Resolution 15, carried by 193 votes against 67, declared that the 'primary and obvious' method to limit or avoid parenthood, where there was 'clearly felt moral obligation' to do so, was 'complete abstinence from intercourse (as far as may be necessary) in a life of discipline and self-control lived in the power of the Holy Spirit'. Nevertheless, where there was 'a morally sound reason for avoiding abstinence', it agreed that 'other methods' might be used, 'provided that this is done in the light of the same Christian principles'. It condemned the use of such methods 'from motives of selfishness, luxury, or mere convenience'. It was this resolution which provoked the papal reply in *Casti Connubii*. In 1958, following upon the publication of a thorough preliminary study entitled *The Family in Contemporary Society*,[14] the Conference, in Resolution 115, asserted the primary responsibility for deciding upon 'the number and frequency of children' as one laid by God upon the consciences of parents everywhere (*sic*), but left the means of planning to their own 'positive choice before God'. In 1968 the Conference contented itself with a courteous rejoinder to the publication of *Humanae Vitae* in a restatement of the 1958 Resolution. The moral reasoning underlying this change, and the process of the change itself, extending over fifty years, will be examined later.

It should be added that the Lambeth Conferences published these resolutions – which have no juridical force, but only that inherent in their own ability to win moral assent – in a context of prescriptions for living the Christian life; Resolution 121 of 1958, for instance, contained a statement of seven 'Marks of a Christian Family' – a loose 'household code' not far removed in content from those embedded in the epistles of the New Testament. The Book of Common Prayer, also, contains rules of fasting and abstinence, alms-giving, participation in public worship and the sacraments, and observance of festival and penitential seasons. In the catechism to be taught between baptism and confirmation, and in the exhortations towards a right preparation for holy communion, it gives firm and clear teaching on the duties of a Christian towards God and towards his neighbour; in particular it enjoins a strict scrutiny of personal disposition and conduct, the confession of sins (before a priest if conscience may not otherwise be quietened), the offering and receiving of forgiveness *vis à vis* the neighbour, and the pursuit of it from God. Until the twentieth century the Ten Commandments have been prescribed for didactic use in the catechism and for liturgical reading in the holy communion; recent revisions have reduced them to the short, ten 'words', or to the Lord's summary of them in the New Testament, or have made their use in the communion service optional altogether. (The Church of England has shared to the full the general confusion about the place of 'law' in morality, and especially about 'negative' prescriptions.) Preoccupation with debatable moral issues is only a sporadic activity: it is no substitute for regular training in the morality of Christian life.

II

After this narration of some of the facts in the moral tradition of the Church of England, there remains the far more difficult task of elucidating the grounds of the action, the methods by which moral judgments are made and formulated. This subject, too, could be historically treated, for the Church of England did not arise *ex nihilo*, but descended from the Western branch of the universal church; and at the Reformation it had to establish its identity, its existence in relation to the Church of Rome on the one side – busy as it was with its own conciliar reformation, at and after Trent – and to the other non-Roman churches, Protestant and Reformed, on the other. John Jewel, Bishop of Salisbury, and Richard Hooker, Master of the Temple, were the principal architects of that identity; and it is in Hooker that the foundations of the moral tradition of the new Church of England are laid down.

Hooker's treatise, *The Laws of Ecclesiastical Polity*, was primarily a defence of the government and liturgy of the Church of England against Protestant and Puritan objections;

in particular he had to defend it against the charges of over-identification with Rome, a task which he accomplished by asserting the validity of *reason* and *tradition* in the formation of judgments, not simply alongside of scripture, but in some sense as the essential context in which and the means by which scripture may be rightly interpreted. Thus where the practice of the Church of England was impugned as 'popish' (e.g., IV.iii.1), its being 'of reasonable continuance' (V.xxix.5), that is, both 'reasonable' and 'of long and accepted use' (IV.iv.1) was a good defence, provided that it were 'not contrary' to the express word of scripture. So through Hooker, the exercise of 'moral reasoning' was established in the Church of England, as against *sola scriptura*, arbitrarily chosen and interpreted, as an infallible guide in every particular of life. The selection of quotations from such an extended work must of necessity be arbitrary; but here are some. In a discussion of *choice*, as compounded of *knowledge*, informed by *reason* and *will*, he writes:

> Where understanding therefore needeth, in those things Reason is the director of man's Will by discovering in action what is good. For the Laws of well-doing are the dictates of right Reason. (I.vii.4)

Some things reason binds men 'of necessity to observe'; others, 'which are left as arbitrary', it guides them to choose (I.xvi.5). Reason is 'the natural way of finding out Laws to guide the Will unto that which is good':

> The general and perpetual voice of men is as the sentence of God himself. For that which all men have at all times learned, Nature herself must needs have taught; and God being the author of Nature, her voice is but his instrument. (I.viii.3)

> The natural measure whereby to judge our doings, is the sentence of Reason, determining and setting down what is good to be done. Which sentence is either mandatory, shewing us what must be done; or else permissive, declaring only what may be done; or thirdly admonitory, opening what is the most convenient for us to do. (I.viii.8)

> Law rational therefore, which men commonly use to call the Law of Nature, meaning thereby the Law which human Nature knoweth itself in reason universally bound unto, which also for that cause may be termed most fitly the Law of Reason; this Law, I say, comprehendeth all those things which men by the light of their natural understanding evidently know, or at leastwise may know, to be

beseeming or unbeseeming, virtuous or vicious, good or evil for them to do. (I.viii.9)

This 'natural law' may, however, be hidden away or smothered by 'lewd and wicked custom' (I.viii.11; cf. vii.6) – an observation which leads Hooker to treat of rewards and punishments, and the work of reason in framing human laws for the government of societies, an activity into which man is led by his natural inclination towards fellowship (I.x.1).

But reason alone does not bring salvation: scripture teaches that (I.xiii.3), and scripture is *sufficient* for it (I.xiv.1).

Nature and Scripture do serve in such full sort, that they both jointly and not severally either of them be so complete, that unto everlasting felicity we need not the knowledge of any thing more than these two may easily furnish our minds with on all sides; and therefore they which add traditions, as a part of supernatural necessary truth, have not the truth, but are in error. (I.xiv.5)

Traditions, so pressed, are not rejected

only because they are not in the Scripture, but because they are neither in Scripture, nor can otherwise sufficiently by any reason be proved to be of God. (I.xiv.5)

Compare I.xv.4, where he insists that 'to search the Scripture of God' for the meanest of vain and childish trifles is to 'derogate from the reverend authority and dignity of Scripture' and to fall into superstition.

It is an error to think that 'the only law which God hath appointed unto men in that behalf (*sc.*, so that men's actions may tend unto God's glory) is the sacred Scripture':

In reasonable and moral actions another law taketh place; a law by the observation whereof we glorify God in such sort, as no creature else under man is able to do; because other creatures have not judgment to examine the quality of that which is done by them, and therefore in that they do they neither can accuse nor approve themselves. Men do both, as the Apostle teacheth; yea, these men which have no written law of God to shew what is good or evil, carry written in their hearts the universal law of mankind, the Law of Reason, whereby they judge as by a rule which God hath given unto all men for that purpose.

But mere morality is not enough, even for men aware of God as their maker:

> The law of reason doth somewhat direct men how to honour God as their Creator; but how to glorify God in such sort as is required, to the end he may be an everlasting Saviour, this we are taught by divine law, ... So that in moral actions divine law helpeth exceedingly the law of reason to guide man's life; but in supernatural it alone guideth. (I.xvi.5)

> What the Church of God standeth bound to know or do, the same in part nature teacheth. (III.ii.2)

To this he adds human and positive law, 'the law of nations' and 'of nations Christian', as further necessities for the life of public societies, civil or spiritual. These laws must be obeyed,

> unless there be reason shewed which may necessarily enforce that the Law of Reason or of God doth enjoin the contrary. Because except our own private and but probable resolutions be by the law of public determinations overruled, we take away all possibility of sociable life in the world. (I.xvi.5)

Following closely St Thomas Aquinas on the nature of human law,

> Laws human must be made according to the general laws of nature, and without contradiction unto any positive law in Scripture. Otherwise they are ill made. (III.ix.2)

In matters indifferent,

> The choice is left to our own discretion, except a principal bond of some higher duty remove the indifferency that such things have in themselves.... In things indifferent there is a choice, they are not always equally expedient. (II.iv.4)

> It is not the Scripture's setting down such things as indifferent, but their not setting down as necessary, that doth make them to be indifferent. (II.iv.5)

So he rejected the Puritans' claim to *prove* every liberty by the express word of scripture, and quoted St Augustine (*Ep.* 19) against them:

> St Augustine was resolute in points of Christianity to credit none, how godly and learned soever he were, unless he confirmed his sen-

tence by the Scriptures, *or by some reason not contrary to them.*
(II.iv.7)

There is no necessity, that if I confess I ought not to do that which
the Scripture forbiddeth me, I should therefore acknowledge myself
bound to do nothing which the Scripture commandeth me not.
(II.v.7)

So, relying on Tertullian also, he argues that

in the Church a number of things are strictly observed, whereof no
law of Scripture maketh mention one way or other; that of things once
received and confirmed by use long usage is a Law sufficient; that in
civil affairs, when there is no other Law, Custom itself doth stand for
Law; that inasmuch as Law doth stand upon Reason, to allege Reason
serveth as well as to cite Scripture; that whatever is reasonable the
same is lawful whosoever is the author of it; that the authority of
Custom is great ... (ibid).

Is this to build too much on the judgment and authority of
man? By no means: we cannot apprehend even the saving truth
of God in Scripture without it:

For whatsoever we believe concerning salvation by Christ, although
the Scripture be therein the ground of our belief; yet the authority
of man is, if we mark it, the key which openeth the door of entrance
into the knowledge of the Scripture. The Scripture could not teach us
the things that are of God, unless we did credit men who have taught
us that the words of Scripture do signify those things. Some way,
therefore, notwithstanding man's infirmity, yet his authority may
enforce assent. (II.vii.3)

Man's search for certainty is by diverse routes. Our greatest
assurance is 'that which we have by plain aspect and intuitive
beholding'. Where this cannot be had, the mind assents to 'what
appeareth to be true by strong and invincible demonstration'.
When both of these fail, 'then which way greatest probability
leadeth, thither the mind doth evermore incline'. Since Scripture
is received as the Word of God, none of these three 'is thought
so sure as that which the Scripture of God teacheth'. But even
this cannot command blind, unreasoning submission:

Now it is not required nor can be exacted at our hands, that we should
yield unto any thing other assent, than such as doth answer the
evidence which is to be had of that we assent unto. For which cause
even in matters divine, concerning some things we may lawfully doubt
and suspend our judgment, inclining neither to one side nor other;

as namely touching the time of the fall both of man and angels: of some things we may very well retain an opinion that they are probable and not unlikely to be true, as when we hold that men have their souls rather by creation than propagation, or that the Mother of our Lord lived always in the state of virginity as well after his birth as before (for of these two the one, her virginity before, is a thing which of necessity we must believe; the other, her continuance in the same state always, hath more likelihood of truth than the contrary); finally in all things then are our consciences best resolved, and in a most agreeable sort unto God and nature settled, when they are so far persuaded as those grounds of persuasion which are to be had will bear. (II.vii.5)

In Book III, where Hooker opens his treatment of the nature of life in the mystical Body, the Church, he distinguishes in passing the natural virtues proper to men as men:

As for those virtues that belong unto moral righteousness and honesty of life, we do not mention them, because they are not proper to Christian men, as they are Christian, but do concern them as they are men. True it is, the want of these virtues excludeth from salvation. So doth much more the absence of inward belief of heart; so doth despair and lack of hope; so emptiness of Christian love and charity. (III.i.7)

But neither these virtues nor the exercise of reason is without the Holy Ghost:

In the nature of reason itself there is no impediment, but that the selfsame Spirit, which revealeth the things that God hath set down in his law, may also be thought to aid and direct men in finding out by the light of reason what laws are expedient to be made for the guiding of his Church, over and besides them that are in Scripture. Herein therefore we agree with those men, by whom human laws are defined to be in ordinances, which such as have lawful authority given them for that purpose do probably draw from the laws of nature and God, by discourse of reason aided with the influence of divine grace. (III.viii.18)

Thus equipped, the church may provide for new situations as well as maintain custom from the past:

All things cannot be of ancient continuance, which are expedient and needful for the ordering of spiritual affairs: but the Church being a body which dieth not hath always power, as occasion requireth, no less to ordain that which never was, than to ratify what hath been before. To prescribe the order of doing in all things, is a peculiar prerogative which Wisdom hath, as queen or sovereign commandress over other virtues. This in every several man's actions of common life appertaineth unto Moral, in public and politic secular affairs unto Civil wisdom. In like manner, to devise any certain form for the outward administration of public duties in the service of God, or things belonging thereunto, and to find out the most convenient for that use, is a point of wisdom Ecclesiastical. (V.viii.1)

Richard Hooker has been drawn on so extensively because his work is the fount of the moral tradition, as of so much else, in that life which the Church of England was forced, by historical circumstance, to enter upon in ecclesiastical isolation towards the end of the sixteenth century. That the fount was fed from sources deep in the Catholic tradition, as well Thomist as patristic, will be manifest to all who know them. It remains to discuss how the church operates now within the tradition it has received. It would be wrong to claim a uniform, unbroken tradition from Hooker's day to this, as it would be wrong, in a lecture of this sort, to explore the variants on and deviations from it. The Bishop of Ossory[15] and Dr C. F. Allison[16] have both published major studies of the Caroline divines of the generations immediately following Hooker, and of the changes of profound theological importance which were already setting in. British moral philosophy developed a path of its own in the traditions of teaching at both Oxford and Cambridge and in the Scottish Universities, and then elsewhere. The revival of moral theology was more a product of the Tractarian movement, resulting in the establishment of a Regius Professorship of Pastoral Theology in the University of Oxford in 1842, later renamed the chair in Moral and Pastoral Theology. Two of its most distinguished occupants in this century, K. E. Kirk, later Bishop of Oxford, and R. C. Mortimer, until 1973 Bishop of Exeter, searched back into the tradition, patristic, medieval and Tridentine, and produced notable studies. Kirk's *The Vision of God* (1931) is the most comprehensive work of English moral and ascetical theology in this century. But until the tenure (1949–71) of Professor V. A. Demant, this tradition made little contact with the range of social concern which descended from F. D. Maurice, J. M. Ludlow and the Christian Socialists through Bishop B. F. Westcott, Bishop Charles Gore, Henry Scott Holland and C. E. Raven to Archbishop William Temple.

The claims of a social morality adequate for this century expressed themselves in such 'unofficial', non-academic activities
as COPEC (the Conference on Christian Politics, Economics and
Citizenship), the Christendom Group and the Malvern Conference; they found academic expression also in the founding
of a Lectureship in the University of Manchester[17] (elevated in
1970 into a chair), and of the F. D. Maurice Chair of Moral and
Social Theology at King's College, London, in 1967.

One other stream of influence has been important enough to
claim attention. In the eighteen-seventies the British Government, alarmed at the incidence of venereal disease, especially
among the soldiery, attempted, by means of the Contagious
Diseases Acts, to licence and regulate prostitution, for the first
time in English history, and in a manner offensive to liberty.
Opposition was mobilized, single-handed at first, by one of the
great women of Victorian England, Mrs Josephine Butler. She
forged into a strange and sometimes uncomfortable alliance the
forces of the women's emancipationist movement, utilitarian
philosophy, the universities, politicians – and the church. She
succeeded, and the Acts were repealed. More, with the help of
W. E. Gladstone and the women's religious communities, she
moved the church to organized and enlightened care for girls
and women then ostracized from society for sexual mis-
demeanour or misfortune. A central body to co-ordinate this
work became eventually the Church of England Moral Welfare
Council. Until it was virtually extinguished by ecclesiastical re-
organization in the nineteen-sixties this body pioneered, notably
in the work of Dr D. Sherwin Bailey, studies of the moral, pastoral and social aspects of sexual behaviour at a depth reached
in no other centres of learning in Britain at the time. To this
body, therefore, was entrusted the task of preparing material
for the Lambeth Conference of 1958 on the related problems of
population growth, economic and social resources, and the
morality of contraception. The Report which its expert Committee produced, *The Family in Contemporary Society*, has
been said by I. T. Ramsey, late Bishop of Durham, and formerly
Nolloth Professor of the Philosophy of the Christian Religion
at Oxford, to represent 'the beginning of a new era in Christian
moral thinking'.[18] It may be studied as a model of the way in
which the Church of England has most recently formed and

commended significant moral judgments.

The first concern of the Committee was to establish, to the best of its ability, the relevant empirical basis of the questions to be examined: demographic, economic, social, industrial and cultural factors, not in Britain only, but also in all regions within the pastoral oversight of the bishops of the Anglican Communion; and the relevant physiological and medical studies. (Some preparatory studies were written in other regions also and were co-ordinated by the Committee.) A sub-committee of theologians and moralists was charged with an examination of these data in the light of the relevant theological traditions. The work of the sub-committee was printed, with the empirical studies, in the lengthy Appendix to the Report.[19] Its first task was to formulate a method of moral reasoning appropriate to an era of rapid social change, an era which presented the Christian conscience with problems of a nature and dimension unknown ever before, and with medical and other knowledge and technology never before at man's disposal. Working as they did in the tradition of Richard Hooker as illustrated above, its members could not expect to find relevant moral prescriptions ready-made, either in the word of scripture or in the Christian tradition, however venerable; they were bound to seek their norms by a moral reasoning which related the claims made by the empirical data to the claims of God upon man, in his marital and family life and in society, as evidenced in scripture and the tradition. They offered three specimens or examples of such moral reasoning, with a commentary upon them.

The first began with the assumption that the metaphysical significance of coitus is attached to a 'given' structure of the act, and then asked whether the introduction of contraception into the act is, in fact, to counterfeit it, and so to deny it metaphysical significance; it concluded (p. 137) that:

> The modified act, though ontologically different from coitus during natural infertility, may on occasion be *morally equivalent*, being the best symbol of love and union that is eligible in the circumstances.

The second exercise re-examined the traditional categories of the 'ends' and 'properties' of coitus, and argued that since coitus 'inevitably serves different ends on different occasions', contraception finds its justification in the nature of the marriage

relationship itself in which there must be responsible use of
human freedom. The third example, starting from only 'the
broadest background of Christian doctrine', simply examined
a case in which man and wife 'conscientiously decided that in
their particular circumstances the use of contraceptives can be
made part of the offering of their marriage to the glory of God'
– and then considered objections to their decision; it concluded
that none was sufficient to invalidate their claim to valid insight.

Bishop Ramsey, reflecting twelve years later upon these exercises in reasoning, wrote of the work as 'an articulation of a
moral claim developed within a wider theological context'; 'the
status of the theology used in the argument was subordinate to
the moral claim which, in one way or another, it was endeavour-
ing to articulate'.[20] It was in fact the case that the Lambeth
Conference of 1958 did no more – and no less – than reduce into
the terms of a Resolution (with supporting argument elsewhere)
a moral judgment already made, tested and acted upon by
Christian husbands and wives, episcopal and clerical as well as
lay, for years before; they had, despite ecclesiastical discourage-
ment, admitted contraception into their married life and could
not convict themselves of sin in having done so. The importance
of the 1958 Report and Resolution, therefore, is that it exempli-
fies an instance in which the *magisterium* of the church formulated and ratified a moral judgment made by a sort of *consensus
fidelium*, for which a good theological justification was worked
out *ex post facto*. That *consensus* which, in the history of doctrine, has been claimed as the forerunner of dogmatic formula-
tion, is here claimed as a source of moral insight which a church
may, and indeed must after testing, properly make its own.

Resolutions of the Lambeth Conference have no juridical
authority; they are statements of the mind of the episcopate
of the Anglican Communion; their authority is that of their
moral persuasiveness alone. Thus Resolution 115 of 1958 affirms
a duty – to subordinate procreation to responsible decision – and
a liberty to choose such means to this end as conscience, in view
of the particular circumstances of the marriage, shall decide.
The duty no one, presumably, would now deny: the liberty,
however, some, priests and people, might still dispute. They are
free to do so: no censure would lie against a priest who preached
against the tenor of the Resolution; though in the giving of

pastoral counsel, whether in confession or outside it, it would be improper for him to suppress the Resolution or to charge with sin the conscience of any person who had in conscience acted on the liberty which it conveyed. In practice, however, the debate has moved on in the intervening years: consciences are less exercised now by the general liceity of contraception – that is very widely accepted – than by the expediency of particular methods, for example hormonal anovulant preparations, which, though warranted as 'safe' and harmless on a very wide statistical scale by all the tests so far formulated, constitute nevertheless a known risk to a minute, and unidentified, statistical minority, and may conceivably entail other risks, the nature of which has not yet been realized, and which have not therefore been tested for in research. The moral question involved here is, what degree of empirical uncertainty is tolerable in framing a course of action in which no known course is without ambiguity? Guidance for questions such as these will come only from inter-disciplinary study of the sort which did the preparatory work for the Lambeth Conference of 1958 – work which, incidentally, drew on the professional experience of civil servants and administrators, because the morality of personal decision had to be considered within economic and social contexts which, in the modern world, are governmental responsibilities; and some of the moral imperatives uttered by the Conference would certainly require governmental action for their realization.

III

From this outline of the moral tradition of the Church of England, of the organs by which the study has been maintained, and of some examples of its specific activity, some summary conclusions may be drawn. The moral training of members of the Christian community is part of their general training in Christian living. It rests primarily upon *tradition* within specific, recognizable communities – families, schools, parishes or other church-centred communities. The communities must be small enough for membership to be perceptible, but so interrelated that the life of the great church flows into and through them, as through a body of which Christ is the Head. The model of Ephesians 4.15-16 is apt. The communities are not isolated from secular society, but are penetrated by it, and penetrate it in return. The medium of specific moral training within these communities is generally the holy scripture, read liturgically, and expounded in sermons, catechetical instruction, group discussion, etc. In common usage, the scripture is appealed to and employed to commend moral positions already maintained, or being developed, within the tradition: it would be unusual in any human society to approach the scripture, as with an 'open mind', and to try to draw from it a moral code or set of ethical prescriptions.

Academic speculation upon the relation of the moral code to scripture produces, as may be expected, a diversity of interpretations. Since the Apostle Paul and the Johannine writings, the most comprehensive interpretation is one of 'response': Christian living, in terms of relationships and activities of love, is a 'response' to the relationship and activity of love revealed by God in the life, death and resurrection of Jesus Christ.[21] The imitation of God in Christ is a variant upon this theme, which has a long tradition in the literature of devotion.[22] The search for answers to specific questions of personal and social ethics in the words of Jesus – a search which appears to be made more readily and hopefully in an age when a young, ethically sensitive and critical generation lives most of its life outside the life of the church community, yet, despairing of the policies of the secular 'establishment', looks eagerly for confirmation of its ideals in whatever 'scriptures' are to be found, Christian and Maoist alike – carries us into the heart of the study of Christian ethics. The Church of England, at the Reformation, formally renounced the doctrine that specific words of Jesus could be treated as legislative norms for a civil society; the last three of the XXXIX Articles of Religion affirm that 'it is lawful for Christian men, at the commandment of the Magistrate, to wear weapons and to serve in the wars'; that 'the Riches and Goods of Christians are not common, as touching the right, title and possession of the same'; and that 'Christian Religion doth not prohibit, but that a man may swear when the Magistrate requireth, in a case of faith and charity'. It is singular that, given this formal position, the resolution of the problem of divorce has been so tied to the supposed express word of Jesus, legislatively interpreted.[23]

Resort to an academic solution of the 'interim ethic' type leaves the practical moralist without guidance for the present or the future. He is better served with an interpretation which, with St Paul (Rom. 13.12), sees the teaching of Jesus as an ethics for the dawn, for the day that is breaking but is not yet here; so as the dawn breaks, we are to leave the ways of the dark, departing night; as it becomes *possible* for us to obey any of our Lord's precepts, it becomes an *obligation* for us to do so; we may not refuse it without apostasy. A 'key' of this sort is certainly useful in relating the highest insights, e.g., into marriage as essentially and exclusively monogamous, to the emergence of a people from a state of society in which polygamy had been demographically, economically and socially the only practicable marital arrangement. The Christian life thus takes its place in a revelation which is understood in terms of historical process – 'a process not yet fully completed but open to a future that is already "anticipated" in the teaching and personal history of Jesus'.[24] The moral tradition of the Old Testament, it should be observed, is not ignored or repudiated in this interpretation: it finds its place in the historical revelation, in the whole background of assumptions before which alone the teaching of Jesus and of St Paul can be understood; the Decalogue, for instance, lends itself to translation into a fundamental code of ethics for civil society better than does the Sermon on the Mount, and as such it is taught among us.

Already, in this exposition, *reason*, the third ingredient in Hooker's trinity, has been brought in alongside of *tradition* and *scripture*, again in its function of enabling moral judgments to be made out of these ingredients. The exercise of reason is more and more demanded in an era, like our own, conspicuous for the rapid development of scientific knowledge and technical possibilities, and for wide and deeply ranging social changes which result in a repudiation of traditional norms and conventions, and a loosening of the social sanctions, formal and informal, which once supported them. Elements in the traditional moral training as part of the Christian life, directed towards the fulfilment of personality in the vision and fruition of God, come under scrutiny when psycho-analysis (and other methods of psychological investigation), together with neurology and biochemistry, not only affect profoundly our understanding (as we suppose) of human personality but also give us tools by which to influence it.[25] Advances both in military technology and in medical science create ethical problems not faced by mankind before, and the church is called upon to form its mind upon them, to offer both to its members and to responsible persons in civil society some guidance in their responses to the practical decisions and opportunities with which they are faced.

This task demands nothing less than an exercise in *moral reasoning*: Christian men, formed by and aware of the theological and moral tradition of their church, gather, in small companies – the Lord worked with twelve – with practitioners in the relevant disciplines, make themselves fully aware of the facts, the possibilities, the complications, the moral ambiguities, the claims upon conscience, conflicting perhaps, implicit in the issue, and then seek for Christian insights concerning them. The tradition cannot give them specific solutions to new problems, or explicit rules for new situations. The most it can afford is a variety of principles of general application, indicating interests or values to be served, promoted or protected; only moral reasoning, exercised with scrupulous regard to the facts and circumstances in issue, can create apt expressions for specific guidance or direction.

The implementing of this guidance may require, further, the exercise of moral *persuasion*; it may require coercive *regulation* or *legislation*, enacted by the relevant competent authorities – civil, professional, political, or (in so far as it has jurisdiction) ecclesiastical. Thus, in the English debate on reforming the law on abortion, it was possible for such a specialist group to assert:

> If we are to remain faithful to the Christian moral tradition, we have to assert, as normative, the general inviolability of the foetus; to defend, as a first principle, its right to live and develop; and then to lay the burden of proof to the contrary firmly on those who, in particular cases, could wish to extinguish that right on the ground that it was in conflict with another or others with a higher claim to recognition.[26]

Parliament's statutory enactment, in the Abortion Act 1967, violated that principle in the opinion of many, setting a legal norm for civil society at variance with the moral norms of the Christian community within it. Despite the difficulties which arise from this, the church, in the moral guidance given to its members, can commend a principle in general, and from it try to derive a moral decision in its pastoral guidance in particular cases.

The moral reasoning of which so much has been written has, of course, a strongly rational element in it; otherwise it could not be called 'reasoning'. But the term does not always imply a process of logical deduction from a stated principle to a particular application. Sometimes it begins with what, for want of a better term, is called 'insight', or with what Hooker, in a phrase quoted above, called 'plain aspect and intuitive beholding'. In simple, if dangerous, language, it might be said that conscience, or judgment, or a sense of fitness, points to a certain conclusion – or to a set of conclusions – and the function of 'moral reasoning' is to examine it, or them, and to show that they are *not contrary* to the moral tradition, or may indeed exemplify or fulfil it in a way that, though new, is more of a fulfilment than any other possibility open at the time. The danger of error, or of self-deceit, in such a process is recognized, and such insights or intuitive judgments have to be put to the test, in the church, and among ethically sensitive men in civil society.

An instance may illustrate the point. In 1970 a question was brought up for public discussion, in a rather sensational way, about the use of aborted fetuses in medical research. Apart from the well-known Roman Catholic Member of Parliament who brought the matter into the open, churchmen were conspicuously and creditably absent from the number of immediate protestors and purveyors of 'radical' solutions. We needed time for a proper investigation and assessment of the facts. More, we needed time to discern what sort of solution appeared or 'felt' to be right. We could then have begun our task of moral reasoning, to elucidate the nature of the problem, and to indicate what measures should be prescribed for what ends.[27] In fact the Government appointed an expert Advisory Group, under the chairmanship of Sir John Peel, which produced a very useful Report, with recommendations for a code of practice.[28] The matter proved to present no major ethical difficulty.

A comparable account of a church's moral activity given from within, say, the Roman Catholic Church, would in many respects be different: there the *magisterium*, the teaching authority, is much more centralized and invested with coercive power. Certainly it appears, from what is known of the events which resulted in the encyclical *Humanae Vitae* in 1968, that the Church of Rome then came very near the process of validating theologically and authorizing magisterially a practice which Christian experience and insight had already accepted as moral; the Pope's commission on birth control seemed to be following the path which the Anglican pre-Lambeth Committee had trodden before 1958.[29] The encyclical itself disappointed those expectations, with resultant loss of priests and teachers to the ministry of the church and continuing confusion about its authority among many remaining in it – and this despite the variety of interpretations put upon the encyclical by episcopal conferences throughout the world.[30] The resources of the Roman Church look, to an outsider at least, enormous, and they are drawn on by moralists and other thinkers outside the Roman obedience. In this period of ecumenical interchange it is to be hoped that the essay in self-understanding which has been the purpose of this lecture may provoke one from the Roman Catholic tradition, and from other traditions also. The modern world is no place for moralists to walk in alone.

NOTES

1. E.g. The Synodal Constitutions of Peter Quivil Bishop of Exeter, 1287, c.XX, printed in F. M. Powicke and C. R. Cheney, ed., *Councils and Synods*, II, part II, 1265-1313, Oxford 1964. Cf. John Myrc, *Instructions for Parish Priests*, ed. E. Peacock, Early English Text Society 1868; and John de Burgo, *Pupilla Oculi omnibus presbiteris precipue Anglicanis summa necessaria* (c. AD 1385).

2. G. R. Owst, *Preaching in medieval England*, Cambridge University Press 1926.

3. *The Register of Edmund Lacy, Bishop of Exeter 1420-1455*, ed. G. R. Dunstan, vol. III, Devon and Cornwall Record Society, New Series 7, 1967, p. 13.

4. *Provinciale seu Constitutiones Anglie*, Oxford 1679; pp. 93, 322, 329, 347.

5. *Cum enim unum corpus simus in Christo, pro monstro esset, quod duo capita haberemus.* Quoted in Walter Ullmann, *Medieval Papalism*, Methuen 1949, p. 159.

6. The evidence was published in *Sexual Offenders and Social Punish-*

ment, ed. D. S. Bailey, Church Information Office 1956. It should be recorded that the Moral Welfare Council contributed as it did, in the 1950s and early 1960s, to the moral thinking of church and nation because of the stature of its two chief Secretaries, Miss Ena Steel OBE and Miss Eve Kennedy; it was the grace and personality found in these two ladies which drew and held men together to do most of what is recorded in this chapter from this period, and after.

7. *Ought Suicide to be a Crime?* Church Information Office 1960.

8. *Artificial Insemination by Donor, Two Contributions to a Christian Judgment,* Church Information Office, 1960.

9. *Report of the Departmental Committee on Human Artificial Insemination,* Cmnd 1105, HMSO 1960. G. R. Dunstan, 'Moral and Social Issues Arising from AID', in *Law and Ethics of AID and Embryo Transfer,* ed. G. E. W. Wolstenholme and D. Fitzsimons, Elsevier Excerpta Medica, Amsterdam 1973.

10. See *Theology* LXXIV, 1971, Editorial, pp. 1ff.; the Bishop of Exeter on his agreement with the Law Commission, pp. 123f.

11. The work was begun by another Archbishop's Commission, whose Report, *Marriage, Divorce and the Church* was published in April 1971 (SPCK).

12. *Abortion: an Ethical Discussion,* Church Information Office 1965.

13. See G. R. Dunstan, 'Lawful and Expedient', *The York Quarterly,* May 1960.

14. *The Family in Contemporary Society,* SPCK 1958.

15. H. R. McAdoo, *The Structure of Caroline Moral Theology,* Longmans 1949, etc. Further work from him is expected in his Scott Holland Lectures, 1972.

16. *The Rise of Moralism,* SPCK 1966; cf. the Bishop of Ossory's review article, 'The Carolines under Criticism', *Theology* LXXII, Sept. 1969, p. 400.

17. R. H. Preston, 'Twenty Years of Teaching Christian Ethics', *Theology* LXXII, July 1969, p. 305. Cf. his 'The Priest as a Teacher of Ethics in a Plural Society', ibid. LXXI, July 1968, reprinted in *The Sacred Ministry,* ed. G. R. Dunstan, SPCK 1970, p. 54.

18. Ian T. Ramsey, 'Christian Ethics in the 1960s and 1970s', *The Church Quarterly* II.3, Jan. 1970, p. 221.

19. Op. cit., pp. 120-160. Reprinted in I. T. Ramsey, ed., *Christian Ethics and Contemporary Philosophy,* SCM Press 1966, pp. 340-381.

20. *The Church Quarterly* II.3, Jan. 1970, p. 222.

21. See John Burnaby, 'Conduct and Faith', in *God, Sex and War,* ed. D. M. MacKinnon, Collins (Fontana) 1963; G. R. Dunstan, *Not Yet the Epitaph,* The University of Exeter, 1968, ch. IV.

22. See Barnabas Lindars, SSF, 'The Bible and Christian Ethics', and 'Imitation of God and Imitation of Christ', *Theology* LXXVI, 1973, pp. 18off., 394ff. A recent study by J. L. Houlden, *Ethics and the New Testament,* Penguin Books 1973, surveys the whole question in the light of contemporary critical understanding of the New Testament and its exegesis.

23. Among many attempts to unravel this problem, Helen Oppenheimer may be cited, in *Law and Love*, Faith Press 1962, and *The Character of Christian Morality*, Faith Press 1965; cf. also *Marriage, Divorce and the Church*, 1971.

24. Henry Balmforth, *Theology* LXXIII, July 1970, p. 323, reviewing W. Pannenberg et al., *Revelation as History*, 1969. In relation to marriage and polygamy, see Adrian Hastings, *Christian Marriage in Africa*, SPCK 1972, especially ch. 4.

25. See *Personality and Science*, ed. I. T. Ramsey and Ruth Porter (Churchill Livingstone, for the Ciba Foundation, 1971), the work of a group of medical scientists, philosophers and theologians.

26. *Abortion: An Ethical Discussion*, pp. 31f.

27. It was *The Tablet*, a Roman Catholic journal, which published the medical scientist's reply to the politician: Dr Bernard Towers, 6 June 1970, with reasoned editorial support. The material facts were set out in a letter to *The Times*, on 21 May 1970, by Mr Donald Longmore. The moralists' reserve was fully justified.

28. *The Use of Fetuses and Fetal Material for Research*, HMSO 1972.

29. See the documents in P. Harris et al., *On Human Life: An Examination of 'Humanae Vitae'*, Burns and Oates 1968.

30. P. Delhaye, J. Grootaers and G. Thils, ed., *Pour Relire Humanae Vitae: Déclarations Episcopales*; Editions Duclos 1970.

4

Born to Rule

If the moralist is, as I have argued in these lectures, an artificer, a craftsman fashioning the artifact called ethics, he need not fear unemployment. The medical sciences alone – to mention no other – provide him with a host of new capabilities unknown to man before. Knowledge creates possibilities – the thought that a new fact might perhaps modify or remedy a known ill; then it gives power, as techniques and instruments are perfected to hazard the attempt, and attempts begin to succeed. The research practioner bestrides two worlds, the known and the unknown: he is assured in what he knows – the conventions of his science give him that security; yet always he must watch for falsifications of his basic theories, or for organic change in his material, making old certainties obsolete; and still he must experiment, with trial and error, to relate his knowledge to his leading hypothesis and purpose. And this, when he can stop to think about it, must be an exhilarating way of life. The moralist can share that exhilaration if he stands near enough to the scientist to learn a little of what he is doing. In this way his own work will begin: his art is to reason his way towards an ethical understanding and judgment, relating the facts of the case to his own conception of reality, and of humanity as part of reality, and to whatever moral insights, his own or those of others, he discerns in relation to the experience.

I am not sure how readily today the world would recognize the moralist in that description. There is a fairly widespread assumption that he stands nearer to an unscientific public which is said to feel itself threatened by such advances in medical science, and that he will therefore articulate their fear first of all, opposing 'progress' in order to defend interests, values and relationships at risk. That popular assumption might amount even to an 'expectation': his job, it would be said, is to see what the scientists are up to and tell them to stop it. That trap is particularly dangerous for him when it is baited by practitioners out of sympathy with what their colleagues are doing: the medical press (to look no further) can always throw up the odd article or lecture by an eminent doctor who, precisely because of his specialist knowledge, can contrive an alarming list of developing practices, and of what more they might lead to, and conclude with a 'Where will it all end?'[1] The enemies of Galileo baited that trap for Pope Urban VIII; the enemies of Darwin baited it for Bishop Samuel Wilberforce; and both, in full pontificals, fell spectacularly in. Today science journalism and science fiction enflame the public fear. Television, in a way, can exploit it, fascinating its viewers with what to them may be horrific but what to people who work in laboratories and operating theatres are ordinary routine procedures; then an opponent of the procedure, be he doctor or moralist, exploits the gut reaction with a few 'facts' and rhetorical questions, leaving viewers with the belief that they have passed an adverse ethical judgment when in fact they have only been feeling queasy. The moralist, if he is to work at his craft, has to cultivate independence, and some severe self-scrutiny.

And what is his task? It is, briefly stated, to help in the formation of new, interim conventions for new medical practices – *interim*, because some are still in the research and development stage, and because some, now established, may soon be superseded at the hand of even their present practitioners. The conventions must embody ethical judgments shared between the practitioners themselves, their medical colleagues in related disciplines, and the public which provides, not only the patients, but also that co-operation, in the gift, for example, of blood for transfusion and of organs for grafting, without which therapy cannot proceed. Without the confidence given by this shared morality, these mutual expectations, science and society will be in conflict; and unless the morality is well-grounded, both wrong and harm will be done to man.

Popular mythology has its slots ready cut, too, for moralists in their respective traditions. It identifies Roman Catholicism with an uncompromising negative; from the known official rejection of artificial contraception, of abortion and sterilization, it is popularly assumed that moralists in that tradition will judge adversely all 'interferences' with the 'natural' course of events in all that concerns the conception and birth of children. Protestantism, on the other hand, has come to be identified with liberalism: an 'ethics of love' or of 'compassion' is assumed to be capable of justifying any medical intervention which will relieve unhappiness and give people, especially parents, a satisfaction otherwise denied them. There are indeed Protestant moralists, like Dr Joseph Fletcher, of Cambridge, Massachusetts, who have identified themselves with a 'situation ethics' which lends colour, if not substance, to this supposition. But a moment's reflection on the work of two of the most serious and influential thinkers in this field today shows that the popular mythology completely reverses the truth. It is the Protestant theologian, Professor Paul Ramsey, of Princeton, New Jersey, who most polemically rejects the pretensions of science journalists in the USA, and denounces the possibilities in research and development which they predict. It is the Roman Catholic theologian, Fr Bernard Häring, teaching in Rome and Bologna, who unfolds a pattern of philosophy and theology which makes moral reasoning *with* the medical scientist possible and indeed promising.

Both men wrote out of positions of attachment to medical faculties designed to give them the fullest awareness of relevant work. Ramsey, in *The Patient as Person*,[2] studied a wide area of research and practice, and judged it, partly against his own strongly covenantal theology, partly against the established codes of medical ethics, notably the Helsinki Declaration of the World Medical Association, 1964. In *Fabricated Man: The Ethics of Genetic Control* he attacked, not simply the work which geneticists and embryologists are now able to do and are doing, like genetic investigation and screening, artificial insemination by donor, fertilization *in vitro* and embryo transfer, but more intensively the notionally possible procedures which *might* develop out of present work. These might include the replacement of normal parenthood by insemination from semen banks, conducted according to a calculated policy of genetic 'improvement', and even human replication by cloning – the continued multiplication of fertilized cells so as to produce organisms genetically almost identical. The strength of Ramsey's work lies in his reference to declared and fundamental principles grounded in his theology and in the tradition of medical ethics. He defends man as an end in himself, whose interest may not be subordinated, without consent, to any interest outside himself, particularly to the abstract ends of 'the good of humanity', 'the future of the human race', or 'the progress of medical science'. He would allow no proxy consent, especially that of a parent for a child born or unborn, to a procedure not intended directly for the good of that particular patient but only or even primarily for 'research'. He would carry these defences back to the very beginning of life, so that he would reject any experiment in 'genetic engineering', for example the introducing of a virus to modify a defective gene (if it became possible), unless it were already *known* that there were no hazards at all.[3] If there is weakness in his work, it is in his matching the extravagance of claim with extravagance of refutation. Engaged polemically as sometimes he is with speculators rather than with practitioners, he can write of serious men's work in ways which they find unacceptable, almost unrecognizable.[4] In following his speculators, he is insensitive to the distinction between what are notional possibilities in biochemical theory and what is actually foreseeable in practice, either in specifically human biology, or in relation to the totalitarian social control which would be necessary to make widespread genetic interference possible; this distinction was drawn as long ago as 1959 by P. B. Medawar,[5] and as recently as 1970 by Anne McLaren;[6] and still as late as 1973 R. G. Edwards can write: 'Fortunately genetic engineering is so distant that there is no urgency in this debate.'[7] Ramsey's standard of unacceptable risk would appear to be so high as to prohibit, not only medical research, but medical treatment as well; indeed, few of us would risk teaching our sons to drive if we allowed the known grave hazards of the roads to create so strict a moral prohibition. Edwards puts the dilemma plainly:

> An immediate issue with new clinical methods concerns the ethics of human experimentation, for if patients are to benefit, new methods have to be perfected, often with the collaboration of people unlikely to gain from the research.

Where Ramsey stands before the medical investigator with a literally protestant 'thus far and no further', Häring is prepared to sit down and discuss with the investigator how far forward they can go together. Häring describes the moral theologian as 'a mediator between the magisterium and medical field-workers', exerting an influence on both.[8] He shares Ramsey's general principles, but he brings to the discussion the much more subtle penetrations of the ideas of 'nature' and 'humanity' which are found in contemporary Roman Catholic moral theology. The task of theology has been to 'de-sacralize' nature, and especially a 'nature' identified with biological processes, as though 'God's absolutely binding will' can be read from them. In this he dissents from the evident intention of article 10 of *Humanae Vitae*. Biological processes normally serve the good of the total human person; when they do, they are to be followed and further developed; when they do not, it is a human duty to experiment, to search out the means to improve them.

> Responsibility for the world in which men are destined to live together is one of the most sacrosanct duties of man, infinitely more sacred than biological processes.

Today's physician is less a 'servant of nature' than a creative manipulator within the forces of 'nature'.

> We should prefer a creative moulding of the *physis* (nature) to all those changes that happen through lethargy or sloth.... I favour 'planned' change over 'natural' change.
>
> Each intervention or medical provision that helps or enhances the wholeness of the human person is right.[9]

Man's true 'nature', in its empirical reality, has yet to be realized; medical research and intervention are means, within their relevant sphere, towards bringing it into being.

This is Häring's position. It still leaves him the task of deciding which particular interventions are ordered to this end, and what treatment is licit or illicit for any particular patient. Yet it offers a far more promising starting-point than Ramsey's profound pessimism, which can describe many of the proposals for 'man's radical self-modification and control of his evolutionary future' as 'a project for the suicide of the species. The momentum behind them is despair over man as he is.'[10]

Häring writes out of a developing Catholic tradition represented, for instance, by Josef Fuchs, SJ, a teacher in the Gregorian University in Rome. His important book, *Human Values and Christian Morality*, contains in particular two studies entitled 'Human, Humanist and Christian Morality' and 'On the Theology of Human Progress'. In contrast to the Stoic view that man may not 'intrude upon the world, and upon man's reality, because these are sacral and divine', Fuchs writes:

> Christianity has begun to understand ... that the reality of the world and of man is something given into the hand of the human person who, as the image of God, is not forbidden to intrude upon this reality, but is called upon precisely to form it. It is man's task to grasp this world and also his own reality, and to attempt to unfold the possibilities that lie in this divinely created reality.

> The reality we call *nature* is also matter in man's hands to be formed and, one can say, humanized and personalized by him. A human morality in the true sense of the word sees the reality of the world, and sees man in the world as its centre, and sees man as a person. Therefore, this morality requires man to give his own imprint more and more to the world, ... give it the shape of his own self and his own rationality.... For a truly human morality, moral action means nothing other than 'being human', 'being rational'. The whole of reality must be subjected to human reason; man has increasingly to give it rational form ... Every reality, including that of man, is created reality. That, indeed, is the meaning of the world and the task of man in the world, in so far as it is the work of God the Creator.

Then Fuchs faces Ramsey's fear, of man-induced changes in the biology of man:

> It is not only allowed, but it is even the duty of man constantly to make himself more a man, that is, always to develop himself further. ... For God has created man *complete with the possibility of his development*, and indeed of *self-development*.... This is our duty precisely because man, with these possibilities, is dependent upon God his Creator.[11]

Fuchs, too, will not identify man's nature with that part of it which is his biological nature, nor read 'natural law' out of it.

> What man can read directly in physical nature as such is nothing more than facts – to which the *physical* laws of nature pertain ... Which use of these physical laws is morally justifiable cannot be discerned from physical nature as such.... Human freedom in a moral context is not simply subject to the physical laws as such. Rather, they should be made use of by man as a person to proceed with the development of himself and his world along truly human, that is, human-

izing, lines, i.e. to set in motion that possibility of the development of mankind and his world which proceeds from God. Thus it is not the physical law that has to be considered as a moral law and invoked to regulate the free actions of mankind, but the *recta ratio* which understands the *person* in the *totality* of his reality.

The natural moral law is to be understood ... as the ever new and still to be solved problem of being a person of this world.

The invasion of nature, thus understood, the conquering of its limitations, the *artificium*, is an essential part of being human, of humanizing nature's realities, of the transformation of nature into human culture.... Certainly, not every arbitrary invasion, not every arbitrary *artificium* is human culture. The invasion, the *artificium*, must be of such an order as to be worthy of man – as a person in nature and the world – and as to create human values – 'human' understood in the fullest sense of the word – and not non-values. But whether certain invasions ... are to be judged as 'human' or basically 'inhuman' we will often discern correctly in our first 'draft', i.e. at the first attempt at a moral judgment; but it can also happen that experience leads us sooner or later to revise this draft, our moral pronouncement.[12]

Thus Fuchs also comes back to what I called, at the end of my last lecture, insight, and the need for moral reasoning upon what is discerned.

II

This is a theological base, I repeat, from which it is possible to go to meet the geneticist, say, and the embryologist, or the neuro-surgeon and the psychiatrist, and to discuss their *artificia*, the means by which they intervene either to influence the sort of person who is yet to come to be, or a person and a personality already formed and perhaps deformed.[13] Medical scientists might not use this sort of language, but it must be in accordance with some such principle that they develop their skills in genetic screening and counselling, to mention one area of practice. It is now possible to diagnose certain genetic disorders before birth by means of the culture and examination of cells shed from the fetus into the amniotic fluid in which it floats in the womb. The taking of the fluid, by trans-abdominal puncture, is not without risk, to the mother and to the fetus; but risk can be reduced by preliminary sonar exploration, and it may be cut still further by amnioscopy, an examination through a fine telescope. The process could be used for what are, in terms of proportion, frivolous purposes, like the establishing of the sex of the fetus, for reasons unconnected with genetic risk. Practitioners writing on the process, however, are clearly at pains to establish an ethics of the practice which would exclude frivolous use. It would be offered only to mothers for whom there were known reasons to anticipate the possibility of their bearing a child with serious chromosomal aberrations, like trisomic Down's syndrome (Mongolism); or with single gene defects, especially sex-linked recessive disorders, like Duchenne muscular dystrophy and haemophilia, in which a male fetus would have a 50% chance of being affected and a female a 50% chance of being a carrier. The indications would be laid down beforehand for which a termination of the pregnancy would follow in the event of an adverse diagnosis. At first hearing this sounds like another avenue opened for the extension of abortion. In fact, the reverse is the case: properly used it can bring precision to what would otherwise remain a wasteful statistical guess. In one reported study, of 51 consecutive patients referred for amniocentesis, in all except one case the fetus proved to have a normal karyotype – the formal description of the chromosomal pattern; this one fetus was established first by chromatin analysis to be a male, and then by karyotype of the cultured cells to have Down's syndrome; it was aborted. Though other studies report a higher rate of termination, the overall frequency being about 12%, amniocentesis can provide a selective and therefore restraining factor in an age which widely accepts abortion for risk of fetal abnormality.[14] Chromatography and other tests on blood cells taken from a child soon after birth can give early diagnosis of a disorder like phenylketonuria, in order that a remedial diet can be planned as early as possible.[15] Better still, early detection of a carrier mother followed by treatment on a special diet can enable a normal child to be born to her; though the child may be a carrier, and so, if it lives to become a parent, it will hand on the defective genetic strain.[16]

In these simple instances the object of the treatment is the direct benefit of the patient, to whom is owed the primary duty of medical care. The ethical distinction between this and research procedures not designed for the direct benefit of the patient is clearly drawn in such codes of practice as that of the Medical Research Council on 'Responsibility in Investigating

Human Subjects',[17] and that of the World Medical Association in the Helsinki Declaration of 1964.[18] The distinction is insisted on in the literature of the practice; for instance, in the Third Report of the WHO Expert Committee on Human Genetics:

> Genetic counselling, like any other medical service, should be devoted to the welfare of the individual or family seeking advice. The counsellor should not pursue any genetic programme designed to benefit future generations if this programme conflicts with the immediate interests of his patients.

> Research ... can never be considered the main object of the consultant, whose primary concern is the counselling of physicians and their patients.[19]

The possible conflict between the two interests, the immediate personal and family interest and the long-term population interest in the reduction of harmful genes, is clearly faced, and resolved in favour of the former:

> In the present elementary state of our knowledge of population genetics, the possible long-range dysgenic effects of premarital counselling must be disregarded. These dysgenic effects are probably negligible compared with those of modern therapy.[20]

Indeed, despite the persistence of myth-makers, geneticists insist that selective breeding cannot eradicate diseases caused by genetic abnormalities nor even reduce the incidence of these abnormalities to the mutation rate which occurs continuously.[21] Even to attempt to do so on a large scale would be adverse to the human interest which, for its continued evolutionary development, requires the widest possible genetic variety. Even the genes involved in schizophrenia are reported to carry traits beneficial to mankind.[22] (This argument does not rule out all attempts to exclude harmful genes conferring no benefit, provided that the means are ethical, that is, that they regard the actual patients involved as 'ends' and not merely 'means'.) Human beings cannot be bred for single characteristics, as calves can be either for beef or for milk, or battery hens simply for eggs. The geneticist, therefore, may be seen to pursue, in his own proper sphere of knowledge and activity, the enhancement of man in the manipulation and humanizing of nature of which the theologians write. He does not reduce the totality of man to his genetic component; yet he learns more and more of how dominant is that component in the actual, concrete reality of man's being. He does not restrict human inheritance to genetic inheritance. We transmit our gene structure, in its infinite variability, in the process of begetting and conceiving. We transmit also our concept of humanity, embodied in varieties of culture, by social communication, from person to person. Within this concept we include admiration for the perfect and the will to pursue it; we include also compassion for the imperfect, and the will lovingly to care for it. Compassion includes the readiness to prevent suffering, where it can be prevented by proportionate action, as well as the duty to relieve it: the duty, therefore, to intervene where intervention, on the strictest analysis, is indicated to be most effective. Between the geneticist and the theologian there is no essential ground of conflict.

III

I turn now to another area of developing medical practice where the moral theologian has a particular duty to encourage calm analysis in place of unreasoned fear. I refer to the fertilization of human ova *in vitro* and their implantation in the uterus. In the eighty-two years since the work of Heape with an Angora rabbit and a Belgian hare doe, an enormous amount of experience and knowledge has been gained in the manipulation and fertilization of ova, and the transfer of embryos, in many mammalian species. The experiments have been marked by a high rate of success, by the rarity of the occurrence of birth defects – nowhere is there reported an incidence above the normal levels – and the remarkable resistance to teratogenesis (the inducement of disorders) shewn by embryos before implantation. It seems that in the early stages of mitosis or cell-division, damaged or defective elements in the cell are reproduced very readily; it is only after implantation, when differentiation has begun, that cell death cannot be made good.[23]

It is well known, of course, that the transition from other mammals to man is highly complicated: what is possible with the one may not be possible, or may not yet be possible, with the other. The fertilization of human ova *in vitro* is now a regular occurrence, and a successful implantation may occur at any time. My sources are the published work of P. C. Steptoe, R. G. Edwards and J. M. Purdy in Oldham and Cambridge and the observed work of D. C. A. Bevis in Sheffield.[24] If I simplify the complexity of their work in my description of it, I know that that will not be taken to imply any lack of admiration or respect.

Spermatozoa are taken from a husband and capacitated, that is, cultured in a suitable medium until they are capable of functioning in the way required. An oocyte is taken from the ovary of the wife, who has been suitably prepared with gonadotrophic hormones, at the time of its optimum maturity before ovulation. Spermatozoa and oocyte are placed together in a suitable culture medium, and the normal random assault on the ovum occurs. One sperm penetrates to the inner nucleus of the egg and other spermatozoa are excluded. Nuclei form from the chromosomes of the sperm and egg, some twelve hours after semination, and then fuse together, as the time for cleavage of the egg approaches. The egg then divides into two cells, then into four, so that by five days or so there are many cells ordered into an early embryo composed of membranes and embryonic region, together forming the so-called blastocyst. The object of the clinicians is to return the fertilized cell to its mother as soon as the difficulties of implantation are understood and overcome. Thenceforward the growth of the embryo would be monitored like any other, by ultrasonic sounding, and later by amniocentesis, and clinical decisions would be taken according to need.

Why is this done? What is the motive? In so far as this is a work of science, the motive is curiosity: the desire to know. First, to know what actually happens in the process of fertilization itself; then, to use the product for research into recesses not otherwise accessible. In so far as this is a work of *medical* science, the motive is to acquire *useful* knowledge: to study early embryonic growth, for instance, with a view to detecting the origin of disorders and to find, perhaps, the means to correct or prevent them. In so far as this is a work of medical *clinical practice*, it is to help a fertile woman, rendered childless by a pathological condition of the oviducts, to become the mother of her own and her husband's child.

The process raises fears, alarms, which we should note though we need not share them. Some rest on crude misunderstanding, as though the laboratory method would ever replace, for any but a tiny minority of mankind, the normal, pleasurable, manner of begetting; or as though the 'test tube baby' would grow up in its test tube, like a schooner in a bottle in the tourist shops at Clovelly or St Ives. There is sensational writing about the 'artificial placenta' in which the embryo would be nourished synthetically until it came to term; but this *is* science fiction, and an economic fiction too. Neither can the possibility of abuse of the process be denied. But in no area of our common life do we stay ourselves from use because of the fear of misuse. Our first task is to work out the ethics of use: we shall then see more clearly what is abuse, and prepare to guard against it. I return to my quest for a language which is meaningful to theologian and scientist alike.

Much of the language used will not help us far. Phrases like 'the sanctity of human life', 'the sacredness of personality' and 'the immortality of the soul' are used with the assumption that they lay us under moral obligation. They may, when we understand what they mean, but with no precision: they do not tell us what we may do, or may not do, in embryonic research; we have to work that out for ourselves by moral reasoning. It is assumed, also, that there are inherited moral certainties, and that they rest on philosophical and theological certainties also – as, for instance, that from 'the moment of conception' the human embryo possesses or becomes 'a living soul'. That certainty, alas, is mythical. It is hardly apt to speak of a 'moment' of conception. Conception is rather a process, beginning with the quick passage of the sperm into the cytoplasm of the ovum and extending surely over the first week of cell division. Moreover popular language about 'soul' and 'body' as two entities is not traditional Christian language at all; it came into the Western tradition through Platonism from remote primitive sources. So long as the Aristotelian tradition dominated Christian thinking, the notion of 'immediate animation' would have been repudiated: animation, too, was a process, and a lengthy one. For the Aristotelians, *psyche*, *anima*, meant, not an entity called 'the soul', but the principle of organization, that which gave a 'thing' and its activities their characteristic form, 'the first principle of life in living things about us'. 'The range of activities of a living thing reveals the kind of soul which is present within it,' writes

Fr Copleston, interpreting St Thomas Aquinas.[25] So a plant has a 'vegetable' soul; animals have 'sensitive' souls; human beings, capable of thinking and choosing freely, have 'rational souls'. The rational soul is what declares the body to be a human body, and soul and body are one substance. The male becomes this, is 'animated' (so the theory went), having traversed the lower stages, at thirty to forty days of fetal life; the female, at sixty to eighty days – a time scale which, in various guises, was to have much importance in the moral and canonical traditions, and even in the English common law tradition, when it became identified with 'quickening'.

Today we may suppress our wish to laugh at this ancient lore – especially in a generation which improperly calls a decerebrate patient a 'vegetable'. Bernard Towers, an embryologist, has remarked that the Aristotelian theories matched empirical observation, pre-microscopic, but apt. Modern embryologists speak of a human embryo becoming a fetus 'when it acquires a recognizable human form', about 3 cms long, at the end of the seventh week, at about forty-five to forty-nine days. Sex can be determined visually at 5 cms, when the phallic tubercle permits identification, at about eighty days.[26] We can claim, therefore, from the tradition, that the recognition, or rather attribution, of humanity has been linked with the phased development of the fetus as empirically observed – and I shall derive more significance from the Aristotelian language in a moment – but we cannot be more certain in the tradition than this. Undoubtedly the full *potential* for human personality is present chromosomally from the time of fertilization, from the fusing of the sperm and the egg. But as we do not know at what precise point in the five million years the anthropoid ape became man, so we do not know at what point in the nine months in the womb the conceptus becomes 'human'. We have to reckon, anyhow, with the estimate that 30%, perhaps up to 50%, of zygotes, fully fertilized human cells, are lost before implantation. Humanity is an attributed status: an imposition from the humane cultural tradition upon the genetic inheritance. It does not follow automatically that we can read off detailed moral rules from the attribution; we have still to work them out for ourselves.

We need a language which does justice both to the theological understanding of 'humanity' and to the embryologist's understanding of the body's development. Only then shall we be able to formulate the ethics of creating a human zygote, experimenting with it, killing it, or letting it die; only then can we examine the question, when does the developing embryo acquire human rights in the sense that it has a claim on clinical care, having an interest of its own which may not ethically be invaded or neglected in the interest of research? I approach the quest for that language in two stages. The first is in biblical terms.

God, we say, is the Creator, continually, the source and giver of life. He creates man 'in his own image'; that is, with a potential for an identity capable of awareness of God, capable of a freely-willed response to the awakening or call of God, and therefore capable of a consequent likeness with God, of being stamped with his mark, his 'character', his image. This capacity for response is a key point in the formula which I shall develop later for the fetus. These beliefs about man, derived from the Old Testament, were confirmed for Christians by the incarnation of the Son of God, who, in Jesus, 'became man', took this human identity, and revealed the image of God in man, exhibiting the total and perfect human response to the moral claim of God. It follows from this that, while all life is to be respected, human life is uniquely precious to God and is to be accounted for, by each man for himself, and by anyone who violates the life of another man. So from this principle, that human life is uniquely precious, we may derive a first moral rule: it is that we are not to procreate life irresponsibly, either by natural process within marriage or outside it, or by laboratory experiment. We shall then have one elementary criterion to distinguish between the use and the abuse of this relevant knowledge: it lies in the responsibility, the personal integrity in aim and method, which the worker brings to his task of bringing together sperm and ovum in a test tube.

From the language of the image of God and the bearing of that image bodily by Jesus Christ his Son, it follows that characteristically human life consists in a mutuality of relationship. Personality is characterized, first, by a capacity for freedom and self-determination, developing as the organism develops its physical and psychological maturity; and secondly by a capacity for mutuality or interaction – a capacity, on the one hand, to make human gestures, on the other to awaken human responses.[27] The old language of 'sanctity' and 'sacredness', used to express the fears evoked by experimental medicine, can now be clothed again with meaning. The words point to the moral notion of inviolability: because the relationships of which this human, psycho-physical organism is the source and centre are ultimately (that is, before God) precious, and therefore ought not to be violated, the psycho-physical source of them, the living body, is itself inviolable. It has an inherent right to be protected; and anyone who seeks to invade that right, to assault, harm or kill that body at any stage, must prove his justification for doing so.

Does this language help us in the search for moral rules in the process of fertilization *in vitro*, for the point where scientific experiment, the legitimate search for knowledge, must cease because it begins to violate a human claim? Is there a point when, granted the possibility, to maintain the life of a human organism outside the womb would become morally intolerable? In order to answer that question, I wish to know whether there is a point, presumably related to the neural development of the fetus, at which the fetus becomes relationally dependent on its mother – dependent on her, that is, for more than a chemical environment, oxygen, nutrient fluids, hormones and the like, dependent on her as a person? When does her *presence* to the fetus begin to awaken in the fetus the potential for human response, as awareness of the fetus begins to awaken in the mother the beginning of a *maternal* response? If we could know at what point a mother, as a human being, as a source of specifically human relationship, becomes irreplaceably necessary to the development of the human embryo into a human child, then we should see a threshold at which experiment must cease, a step which must not be crossed. For beyond it lies the life of a man, the image and glory of God: and this is holy ground.

I had reached this point in my thinking, which I have called the first stage – and received no answers to my questions from my friends among the practitioners – when I read Bernard Häring's pursuit of the same theme.[28] He too went behind the late theory of immediate ensoulment to the Aristotelian language of process; he too sought to match this to the observed process of development; he even identified the *anima*, the rational 'soul', 'a typically human life-principle', with the contents of the genetic code which will make a particular organism into a unique human being – an identification which I should hesitate to make. He too speculated about the moment of 'relationship', and speculated whether it could be at implantation – ignoring, perhaps, that already, before implantation, the zygote has been the source of hormonal signals to the mother: 'relationship', as I have used the term, is not yet. But at length he built his case on the development of the cerebral cortex, of that which distinguishes man from animals, 'hominizes' him, and this brought him also to somewhere near the fortieth day. From about the fortieth day on there is no *new* initiative, only the unfolding of a potential already latent. He concluded, therefore, in a carefully guarded personal opinion, with some support from Karl Rahner:

> I think it can be said that at least before the twenty-fifth to fortieth day, the embryo cannot yet (with certainty) be considered as a human person; or, to put it differently, that about that time the embryo becomes a being with all the basic rights of a human person.... If this theory [of hominization as dependent on the development of the cerebral cortex] gains general acceptance by those competent in the field, it could then contribute greatly to the resolution of those difficult cases involving conflict of conscience or conflict of duties.[29]

It would not follow from Häring's speculation that the life of the embryo might be terminated, in these early stages, without moral justification; this is the subject of the next lecture. It would appear, however, to lend support to the first stage of my argument, by adding precision to the question put to the clinical embryologist. Would he find here, in the developing function of the cortex, the basis (no more) for a relevant ethics?

It has been my purpose in this lecture to illustrate the task of the moralist in helping to formulate new, interim, conventions in one or two areas of medical practice. It was my intention at the outset to include a treatment of artificial insemination by donor also, but time forbids it. I may perhaps refer instead to a fairly full discussion of the question, in its clinical, legal and ethical aspects, in a new Ciba Foundation symposium entitled *The Law and Ethics of AID and Embryo Transfer* to be published this year.[30] At all events, I hope I have laid some foundations in this study of medical intervention in the beginning of life to consider, in my next lecture, interventions for its termination. There is more than poetic fancy to link man's first with man's last long home.

NOTES

1. E.g. Professor Ian Donald, MBE, MD, FRCS, FRCOG, BA, 'Naught for Your Comfort', *Journal of the Irish Medical Association* 65, 10 June 1972, p. 284.

2. Paul Ramsey, *The Patient as Person*, Yale University Press 1970.

3. Paul Ramsey, *Fabricated Man*, Yale University Press 1970, p. 117.

4. See Ramsey's two articles, 'Shall We "Reproduce"?', *Journal of the American Medical Association* 220, 5 and 12 June 1972, pp. 1346f., 1480f. For rebuttal see R. G. Edwards, 'Fertilization of Human Eggs in Vitro: Morals, Ethics and Law', *Quarterly Review of Biology*, Baltimore, March/April 1974.

5. P. B. Medawar, *The Future of Man*, Methuen 1960.

6. A. McLaren, 'The Biological Regulation of Reproduction', in *The Family and its Future*, ed. Katherine Elliott, J. and A. Churchill, for the Ciba Foundation, 1970.

7. Edwards, op. cit.

8. Bernard Häring, *Medical Ethics*, St Paul Publications 1972, p. 36.

9. Ibid., ch. 5, esp. pp. 53-63.

10. *Fabricated Man*, p. 159. See a further and important discussion in a special number, 33.3, of *Theological Studies* (Baltimore, Maryland, Sept. 1972: cf. 33.4, Dec.), entitled 'Genetic Science and Man'. So, R. A. McCormick, SJ, after a critique of Ramsey (pp. 535ff.), writes (p. 549): 'In the past we were guilty of an individual reading of the principle of totality. The task of contemporary moralists is to do justice to the social, cosmic, aspects of man without falling into collectivism. Contemporary genetic possibilities force on us a realization of responsibilities beyond the individual.'

11. Josef Fuchs, *Human Values and Christian Morality*, Gill and Macmillan 1970, pp. 115-17.

12. Ibid., pp. 143, 184f.

13. See *Personality and Science*, ed. I. T. Ramsey and Ruth Porter, Churchill Livingstone 1971, for the product of a long study of this question by philosophers, theologians and medical scientists in relevant disciplines.

14. M. A. Ferguson-Smith, 'Ante-natal Diagnosis of Genetic Disease by Amniocentesis', a paper prepared for a Working Party convened by the British Association to study the implications of recent advances in genetics; the result of the study, written by Alun Jones and Walter Bodmer, is to be published by Oxford University Press in 1974. Cf. J. H. Edwards, 'Uses of Amniocentesis', *The Lancet*, 21 March 1970, pp. 608f.

15. G. M. Komrower, 'Phenylketonuria: Some Current Problems', *Archives of Diseases in Childhood* 45, 1970, pp. 2-4; and 'Screening

Programmes for the Detection of Phenylketonuria', for which see note 14.

16. A. E. H. Emery, in a paper read to the British Association at Leicester, 8 September 1972. *The Times*, 9 Sept. 1972.

17. *Report of the Medical Research Council for 1962-3*, HMSO, Cmnd 2382, pp. 21-25.

18. Printed, e.g., by G. E. W. Wolstenholme and Maeve O'Connor in *Ethics in Medical Progress*, J. and A. Churchill, 1966; paperback edition entitled *Law and Ethics of Transplantation*. See a commentary on it by a WCC study group in H.-R. Weber, *Experiments with Man*, World Council of Churches, Geneva 1969.

19. *Genetic Counselling*. WHO Technical Report Series, no. 416, Geneva 1969, pp. 13f.

20. Ibid., p. 20.

21. Medawar, op. cit.; A. E. H. Emery and W. Bodmer, see n. 14.

22. R. Eliot Slater, see n. 14.

23. C. R. Austin, 'Transfer of Eggs and Embryos to the Oviduct in Mammals'; see n. 14. See also *The Canberra Times*, 31 Aug. 1973, for a report on similar work in Melbourne.

24. P. C. Steptoe and R. G. Edwards, 'Laparoscopic Recovery of Pre-ovulatory Human Oocytes after Priming of Ovaries with Gonadotrophins', *The Lancet* 7649, 4 April 1970, p. 683. R. G. Edwards, P. C. Steptoe and J. M. Purdy, 'Fertilization and Cleavage *in vitro* of Preovulatory Human Oocytes', *Nature* 227, 26 Sept. 1970, p. 1307. Cf. Patrick Steptoe, 'Clinical Aspects of Collection of Human Ova, their Fertilization and Uterine Implantation', see n. 14; R. G. Edwards, op. cit.

25. F. C. Copleston, *Aquinas*, Penguin Books 1955, p. 154.

26. Bernard Towers, 'Life Before Birth' and 'Man in Modern Science', in *Concerning Teilhard and Other Essays*, Collins 1969.

27. See the expansion of the theme in *Personality and Science*, ed. I. T. Ramsey and Ruth Porter.

28. Häring, *Medical Ethics*, pp. 75ff.

29. Ibid., pp. 84f.

30. *The Law and Ethics of AID and Embryo Transfer*, ed. G. E. W. Wolstenholme and D. Fitzsimons, Elsevier Excerpta Medica, Amsterdam 1973.

5

Dying to Order

Lest in writing these lectures I should wander into fantasy, a honeysuckle bush beneath my study window distracts me into reality. Blackbirds nest there: in a few flurried hours, every year, they go in to build, with birch twigs beaked up from the shrubbery beside the lawn. Then there is silence while the dam sits, broken only by a homely chirrup as the cock hovers discreetly for half a second, before entering with its food. In simplicity is life begun; and no less exhilarating is this beginning for those who watch than the miracle in the test tube, of which I spoke yesterday. No less marvellous is life's preservation. A magpie walks slyly, sideways, across the lawn, as though only by accident was he going to the bush. Once there, he leaps towards the nest; and the silence is shattered, as with piercing alarm the cock dives at him out of the birch, and still dives and harries the marauder until he lumbers away. Later, he will dive shrieking again when the cat comes to crush the fledglings in the early days of flight. What is it, what deep ancestral force, which dictates that life, once begun, is to be so preserved, which drives the blackbird into the very jaws of its own death in order to save its young? And what is happening to man that, all across the world, he can, with less and less of qualm, suppress this deep natural instinct to spare his own kind? We face the problem of clinically inflicted death.

'Liberalism' is a word to be used with caution, partly because of the imprecision attaching both to itself and to that which it is used to denote; partly because it is used as a term both of approval and of disapproval, whether the user likes the attitude of mind described, or not. It is bound up in paradox. And one paradox is this. On the one hand liberalism heightens the value put upon human life: it campaigns against capital punishment;

it is quick to expose any lack of restraint by soldiers acting, as in Ulster, against ruthless terrorists; it protests against the extended use of firearms by the police, even when facing armed criminals; it supports every effort to reduce the devastation of war, from conventions at government level to ban biological or chemical weapons to campaigns against nuclear armaments, or against obliteration bombing or the use of napalm in Indo-China. It leads the world's conscience in a heightened respect for life, and for the quality of life, irrespective of colour, or criminality, or politics, or religion, or any other difference between persons. This on the one side. On the other it leads the campaigns for 'liberalizing' the laws against abortion and for 'legalizing' euthanasia; that is to say, campaigns to promote the clinical infliction of death. This paradox is not the creation of academic fancy: it is clearly evidenced on the pages of 'liberal' newspapers in Britain and probably elsewhere, and in the writings and utterances of 'liberal' churchmen and theologians in Britain and the USA. It becomes the duty, therefore, of one like myself, who would stand with the liberals on one side of their paradox in their respect for life, to scrutinize the arguments for its termination.

I

'Abortion is a serious health problem throughout the world.' I quote a Supplement to the *International Planned Parenthood Federation News* of March 1972, which surveyed the legal status of abortion in 138 countries. Of these, there are only thirty-one in which abortion is still illegal. (South Australia stands in the list with legal grounds for termination; the Canberra House of Representatives declined to enact a Bill for the Australian Capital Territory on 10 May 1973.) This extension is very much the work of the last twenty years. The extension is not in numbers only, but also in grounds for termination, as many as eight in some enactments. The Report continues:

> More than half of the world's population now live in countries where abortion is available for medico-social as well as purely medical reasons. In countries where there is a national family planning programme or where the trend is towards smaller families, the abortion rate (legal or illegal) increases.

This is because, contraception once embarked upon and having failed, the determination not to have another child carries over in the resort to abortion. And where there is little or no contraception, abortions reach a high figure and may even exceed the number of births. The Supplement to the *Studies in Family Planning* published by the Population Council of New York record the spread of abortion as a method of family planning and of population control. Increasingly it is available 'on demand', and with the minimum of formality, in special outpatient centres; the method is increasingly by vacuum aspiration, in early pregnancies; and, as for instance in China, the operation is performed by midwives, with the attendance of a doctor only for late or complicated cases.[1] The line between contraception and abortion is further blurred by the intra-uterine contraceptive device causing rejection of the blastocyst, the fertilized cell; and, presumably, by the sort of pill which has its effect *post coitum*.

In England and Wales the new Abortion Act 1967 came into force on 1 April 1968. Contrary to popular belief, the Act did not create a new right or liberty, to secure an abortion on demand; it defined the limits of legality, declaring that

> a person shall not be guilty of an offence under the law relating to abortion when a pregnancy is terminated by a registered medical practitioner if two registered medical practitioners are of the opinion, formed in good faith:
>
> (a) that the continuance of the pregnancy would involve risk to the life of the pregnant woman, or of injury to the physical or mental health of the pregnant woman or any existing children of her family, greater than if the pregnancy were terminated; or
> (b) that there is a substantial risk that if the child were born it would suffer from such physical or mental abnormalities as to be seriously handicapped.

In the first full year of the operation of the Act, 37,736 terminations were notified. In the last complete year, 1972, so far reported, 159,884 were notified; and of these 100,665 were in private nursing homes or clinics approved under the Act – that is, on payment of fees; only about one third were carried out in hospitals under the National Health Service. The figures prompt the inevitable question: would the numbers have been so high if the Act had forbidden the procurement of an abortion for profit? Over the last five years the British Pregnancy Advisory Service has extended its coverage, offering private patient facilities at a fee high enough only to cover costs, with the avowed aim 'to demote the profiteers';[2] it is doing so with some success.[3] Its statistics show how nearly supply now matches demand: in the last reported year, 99% of women seen by its counsellors were granted certificates for abortion; only 1% were refused, and these included some too far advanced in pregnancy to be considered.[4] (There would have been some preliminary sifting by general practitioners before referral.) As a check or screen it looks as though the Act exercises very little control. The scene is well set for the advent of prostaglandins which, if pharmacological predictions are correct, will remove the decision to terminate in the early stages of pregnancy out of the medical context altogether. Abortion would then be without demand; it could be self-induced.

We are called upon, then, to consider the ethics of a practice already very widely spread, and likely to grow in incidence in all regions of the world, developed and developing. We must begin with the status of the fetus. What is it?

There are two extreme views. At one extreme, the embryo has the status, and therefore the full rights, of a 'human being' from the moment of conception. Since its life is an 'innocent' life, it may not be taken: the law of Moses is quoted in its defence: 'the innocent and righteous slay thou not' (Ex. 23.7). In the Christian tradition, Tertullian is quoted, from about AD 200, as an early witness to this view; though it must be observed, first, that theologians are accustomed to treating Tertullian with much caution on other matters, and secondly, that there is nothing in his statement to tell us at what precise stage in its growth he thought the fetus became entitled to the protection which he accorded to it. This is what he wrote:

> For us, indeed, homicide having been forbidden once and for all, it is not lawful to destroy even that which is conceived in the womb while the life-blood is still being drawn into a human being. To deny birth is to hasten the homicide; for it makes no difference whether you snatch away a life when born or drive it out while coming towards birth. Even the man who is still yet to be is a man, just as every fruit is already present in its seed.[5]

Tertullian did not stand alone among Christian writers at the time, who voiced the common Christian determination to raise the low value put upon unborn and infant life in the pagan world around them.[6] This view remains that of the Roman Catholic Church, which forbids a direct attack upon the fetus; though a relevant casuistry gives Catholic doctors the essential freedom of indirect action in cases of strict medical necessity.

At the other extreme stands the view that the fetus has no independent status; it is no more than a tissue or a cyst upon the mother's body, to be excised entirely at her command. This view underlies the 'liberationist' claim that every woman has an absolute right to decide whether to bear a child conceived in her or not; no such claim could be sustained if it were allowed that the fetus has rights itself.

Can the facts help us to choose between these views, or to formulate another? At the biological level the facts are incontrovertible: the full potential for human life is present from the time when even cell division occurs and the chromosomal formation of the morula is complete, that is, from about day seven. (To place the potential earlier than that would encounter the possibility, and therefore the logical difficulty, of twinning.) The zygote has within itself an identity distinct from that of either parent, though derived from both; already it carries the genetic coding which will result in a distinct and unique person. Physiologically speaking, there is henceforward no point at which a line may be drawn where 'life' begins, or between not being 'human' and becoming 'human': not at implantation, for that is a change, not of inherent constitution, but of environment necessary for viability; not at quickening, for that is a subjective experience of the mother's; not at birth, for that is an event timed more and more by medical decision and action, and neo-natal life is only environmentally different from immediate pre-natal life: another year of human, relational, life – of contact with a mother – is required for the neuro-anatomical connections to be fully made and the nerve centres of the brain to be fully co-ordinated. Every advance in monitoring the fetus confirms its individuality – a distinct heartbeat, a circulation system distinct from that of its mother, a distinctively individual pattern of brain activity, recorded on the EEG (electroencephalogram) at eight weeks. And if we allow the evidence of the EEG at the terminal end of life as an indication that the patient is a 'person' to whom is owed the duty of medical and nursing care, at least it must be allowed to create a *presumption* of that personhood

and of that duty at the beginning of life also: the burden of re-
butting the presumption must lie on those who would dispute it.

Physiologically considered, it is inescapable that the fetus has,
from the beginning, the capacity to become a separate human
person. The law, in fact, treats it as one: the consistent tendency
of the law over the last two decades has been to recognize more
and more rights in the unborn child – except (in the oddest of
paradoxes) the right to life itself. 'Liberalized' abortion legislation runs directly contrary to all other tendencies of the law in
the same period. The decision of the full state court of Victoria,
Australia, in the case of Sylvia Watt, that she can legally sue for
damages on account of brain damage sustained in a car accident
before her birth,[7] is entirely consistent with recent decisions in
the American courts,[8] and with proposals for legislation made by
the English Law Commission, now under study.[9] The American
decisions have kept pace with medical knowledge in recognizing
an independent existence in the unborn child from the earliest
stages of its development, and in imputing to it a legal personality for all purposes which would benefit it after its birth. It
treats the fetus consistently 'as a person, and hence the subject of
rights'. In questions of property and inheritance,

> it is the remedy and not the right that is contingent on the subsequent
> live birth of the child. The unborn child possesses the right, regard-
> less of his subsequent development or arrest thereof.[10]

The time of quickening is irrelevant in this new case law – a notable advance on the old English common law tradition as stated
by Blackstone, that 'life begins in contemplation of law as soon
as an infant is able to stir in the mother's womb'.[11] In tort,
courts grant recovery of damages to the child who has been
harmed *in utero* by negligent injury. On medical care, courts
have held 'that the fetus itself was before the court and was entitled to protection by the state'; that protection could extend not
only to authorizing a blood transfusion immediately after birth,
against the mother's opposition, but also to overriding, in the
interest of her unborn child, a pregnant woman's refusal to receive a transfusion herself, and her right of religious freedom on
which that refusal was based.[12] The Report of a specialist group
set up to advise the British Government on the use of fetal
material for research lays down the same ethical and legal

controls for research on a viable fetus as apply to a human person, and for a non-viable fetus it prescribes stringent controls.[13]

Logically considered, therefore, it would appear that Tertullian's judgment, made about the year 200, is confirmed by today's understanding of embryonic development, and that the law, in extending its protection – in everything except life – to the earliest stages of development is accordant with it. It would appear also that, if we could read off a clear moral duty from so clear an array of physiological facts – a luxury seldom allowed us in other fields of ethics – that duty would be aptly expressed in the absolute prohibitions of the destruction of fetal life in any circumstances, issued by the Holy Office of the Roman Catholic Church in 1884, 1889 and 1902[14] and confirmed in all subsequent papal utterances.

The question before us is, do the facts dictate this absolute duty? or, in other terms, has the fetus, from its earliest existence, an absolute, that is, unqualified, right to protection, to life? Absolute means admitting of no exceptions. If we put an absolute value on human life we mean that in no circumstances may life be taken: that no other consideration may deter us from preserving that life to the utmost of our ability and as long as possible. First we must observe that in our general ethics, even in our general medical ethics, we do not act upon this absolute principle. Good medical practice recognizes that at the terminal stage of illness appropriate management is not to strive by all possible means to keep the patient alive but to comfort and assuage him as he achieves his natural end in death. Leaving aside the disputed questions of capital punishment and killing in war, we have a category known to the law as justifiable homicide. A court will not convict for killing in self-defence, when no other, less drastic, course was available, and when the act of killing was intended, not to end the assailant's life, but to protect the life of the person attacked. Even in England, where there is great reluctance to issue firearms to the police, a policeman who shoots and kills a bandit or terrorist using a firearm is held to act lawfully.

In fact, then, we do not place an absolute value on life in our general ethics; there could be no justification for homicide, ever, if we did. We place a very high value on life; we insist that it is to be preserved and protected; and we lay the burden of proof or of defence on anyone who would evade or deny that general duty. If this be true of human life in its full, conscious development, it would seem odd to place a higher, absolute, value on fetal life with its potential still unformed. We may indeed argue, and in ethics we should, that the weakest, the most vulnerable and defenceless, should receive the greatest protection; but that is not the same as to guarantee absolute protection. If we assert a continuity of life from conception to death, we would seem to be bound to a moral continuity also: to seek a moral formula applicable to fetal life as much as to developed life; in other words, to extend the concept of justifiable homicide back to a concept of justifiable feticide also.

At once an objection rises against this. Justifiable homicide presupposes that the assailant has, by his aggressive act, morally renounced or at least jeopardized his right to protection; the fetus, in contrast, is 'innocent' in the sense that it is still incapable of an immoral, as of a moral, act. The objection would be well-founded, were it not that the concept of justifiable homicide applies also to the death of an assailant who, because of mental impairment and hence of diminished responsibility, would not be held morally culpable or legally guilty of the attack. Moreover, it is true that, in the very moral tradition which sought to uphold the principle in 'the innocent and righteous slay thou not', protection was matched to development, higher with fetal growth, lower in the earlier embryonic stages. The Aristotelian tradition of delayed 'animation' which has been mentioned earlier – thirty to forty days for a male fetus, sixty to eighty for a female – gave a philosophical grounding for this discrimination. Gregory of Nyssa, writing at the end of the fourth century about belief in the Holy Ghost, uses the distinction between 'fully human' and 'potentially human' as a premiss – and therefore assumed to be understood and acceptable – for another argument:

> For just as it would not be possible to style the unformed embryo a human being, but only a potential one – assuming that it is completed so as to come forth to human birth, while as long as it is in this unformed state it is something other than a human being – so our reason cannot recognize as a Christian one who has failed to receive, with regard to the entire mystery, the genuine form of our religion.[15]

The Irish Penitentials, which so powerfully influenced the moral tradition of Western Europe, graded the severity of their penances on the same basis:

> The penance for the destruction of the embryo of a child in the mother's womb, three years on bread and water. The penance for the destruction of flesh and spirit [i.e. the animated fetus] in the womb; to do penance for fourteen years on bread and water.[16]

The distinction between *fetus animatus* and *fetus inanimatus* or *informis* persisted unbroken in the Roman Catholic tradition until the decrees of 1884 to 1902 – except for three years between the issue of an 'absolutist' decree by Sixtus V in 1588 and its revocation by Gregory XIV in 1591. Absolute protection for the fetus at every stage has not been guaranteed for any but a very short time in the Christian moral tradition.

This is not to assert, however, that feticide may be without justification. The burden of proof must be a very heavy one; and it must rest on the notion that the fetus is an aggressor, however innocent, an invader of another interest adjudged to have a higher claim to protection, no less drastic remedy being available, so that the death of the fetus would be unavoidably and incidentally incurred in meeting that claim, and not intended directly in itself. To defend a midway position such as this is a far harder task than defending an absolutist position – logically, at least, whatever practical difficulties the absolutist encounters; it is nevertheless a moral necessity if justice is to be done to the whole complex of claims and principles involved. We have yet to see what comfort it affords us in our present world predicament.

What sort of claim might be held to justify feticide? Of the seven or eight commonly found in the laws permitting abortion, I select three for comment. First comes the medical indication of a risk – 'grave', 'serious', 'substantial', or similarly described – to the mother's life, or to her physical or mental health. This was, roughly speaking, the case law in England between the Bourne judgment of 1939 and the Abortion Act of 1967. The conflict of claims between mother and fetus has been so much argued as to require no further treatment here.[17] But observe: in countries where medical science is advanced, these medical indications, strictly determined, become less and less. With the advance of skill in treating adverse conditions of the heart and kidneys and other complications, and in early induction of labour where necessary, the risk of death or disablement in childbirth is less than ever before. The latest figures published in England and Wales, those for 1971, shew a maternal death rate of 17 per hundred thousand total births, the lowest ever – a decline from 53.3 per hundred thousand in the years 1952-1954.[18] 'Abortion remains the largest single cause of maternal deaths, as it has since 1958' – despite the decline in the number of deaths from abortion also; I quote an official report from the Department of Health and Social Security.[19] It seems disingenuous to continue to play up the risks of normal childbirth, while playing down the risks of abortion, including the risk of morbidity or impaired fertility thereafter. And if this is true of advances in the care of physical health, one might hope that it were true also of advances in the psychiatric and social care which contribute to mental health, and which could reduce psychological risks also in childbirth. In terms of strict 'necessity', therefore, it seems that the threat to maternal life or health, while undoubtedly present in some cases, is of declining general force. So it is the more remarkable that in England and Wales in 1971 the majority of abortions notified, 76.4%, were alleged to fall under Ground 2, 'that the continuance of the pregnancy would involve risk to the physical or mental health of the pregnant woman greater than if the pregnancy were terminated'. It is even more surprising that, of all *single* women aborted on medical grounds in 1971, 94.5% were stated to be suffering from 'mental disorder': a diagnosis which most of us as lay persons would hesitate to make of most of our unmarried pregnant friends and acquaintances.

The second indication is the risk of congenital handicap in the child if born; a 'substantial' risk, the English Act says, and the handicap has to be 'serious' – and rightly so if the threat is to be counted as grave enough to justify feticide. Some distinctions must be drawn. First, the termination may be considered either in the supposed interest of the child – that it is thought 'better' for him that he should not live at all than live with a foreseeable handicap – or in the 'interest' of those who would have the care of him, and to whom he would be a 'burden', or who might feel more sorry for him than he would feel for himself. Secondly, there is a difference between diagnosis (or prognosis) and statistical risk. Apart from those few chromosomal disorders (like trisomic Down's syndrome) or enzyme deficiencies that can be positively diagnosed by amniocentesis, and those (like gross hydrocephaly) which can be diagnosed only very late in pregnancy, the most that can be predicted is a statistical risk of defect – as high as 50% for the rare conditions, like haemophilia (if the fetus is male), but much lower for other disorders, like those arising from maternal contact with rubella. To terminate on the basis of statistical risk is to accept the necessity of killing more healthy fetuses than defective ones. Fortunately, again, scientific advance reduces the area of uncertainty: 80% of adults are immune from rubella, and antibody tests on a mother known to be in contact can determine whether she is immune or not; and the prospects of intra-uterine diagnosis of other disorders look like improving. Medical possibilities point to more discrimination, not less.

And what of the handicapped child if born? Technological advance makes this world steadily more hospitable for him, not less, if we have the will to use it. Prostheses (artificial aids to support and movement) advance in ingenuity; well-designed furniture increases mobility, comfort and stability; push-button technology makes it possible for severely handicapped people, even with impaired mental capacity, to work economically. All this, with extended medical, social, and educational services, offers a degree of support to handicapped life, and of fulfilment within it, unavailable before – if we have the will to use it. If, nevertheless, we terminate, let us be clear what we have decided. We have decided to back the pursuit of physical perfection (which we can never achieve) by working within the mechanics of biological inheritance; we have decided not to back the enhancement of specifically human, or humane, characteristics carried within our cultural, non-genetic inheritance; and these include the accumulated ethics of care, compassion, tolerance, mutuality of giving and receiving, the intelligent application of mind and knowledge to the relief of suffering. We deny ourselves the experience of *being humanized*, by the trust and generous affection, say, of a Mongol person. We replace a tradition of mutual care with a tradition of disposal. We pass from the question, what harm are we doing to the fetus by destroying it, to the question, what harm are we doing to ourselves, to humanity, when we do so?

This question becomes the more pressing when we turn to the last legal ground which I shall consider, that, included in the English Abortion Act of 1967, which extends the threat to the life or health of the pregnant woman to 'any existing children of her family' – a threat which must be 'greater than if the pregnancy were terminated'. (In 1971, 3.3% of abortions notified were on this ground.) I must ask: given the wealth of the country which enacted that clause – wealth in terms of medical, social and economic resources – what sort of threat can this be, which cannot be met by other and less drastic means than the termination of fetal life? And is it capable of medical diagnosis? Two registered medical practitioners have to determine it: how can they form a medical opinion on such a matter 'in good faith'? A threat to convenience, or to hopes or expectations or style of life, all this can be envisaged; its assessment would be more proper to a social worker than to a doctor. But can a *nuisance* of this sort, however severe, admit of no other remedy than feticide? Does *this* constitute justification, in terms of the normal ethics governing the protection of life?

In fact, the main clauses of this act entrench an historic muddle, the result of political compromise. Subsection (2) of the Act, following upon the recitation of grounds for termination recited in subsection (1), declares that

> In determining whether the continuance of a pregnancy would involve such risk of injury to health as is mentioned in paragraph (a) of subsection (1) ... *account may be taken of the pregnant woman's actual or reasonably foreseeable environment.*

The words italicized were taken, almost *verbatim*, from a draft Bill put up for consideration by a Church of England Committee, but so taken out of context as to vitiate their intent. The Church committee insisted that the one ground which could justify termination should be a 'grave risk of the patient's death or of serious injury to her health or physical or mental well-being'.[20] All other considerations – risk of congenital handicap, or conception as a result of rape or other offence – would be considered circumstantially, as factors bearing on this one relevant matter of medical judgment, the prognosis for the mother. But so insistent was the Church committee that this judgment should not be taken in a vacuum, but rather should refer to the woman as she was, with all her difficulties (or none), that it wrote this 'environmental' clause into its draft Bill. The main clauses of the Bill went some way in Parliament. Then, when Parliament extended the grounds, so destroying the logic of the Church Bill, it kept the environmental clause in a context for which it was not intended, so compromising the Church of England with an enactment to which its Bishops, with one exception,[21] were in principle opposed. This item of domestic history is recalled by a participant in it as a warning about what might happen in other legislatures.

It would appear, therefore, that the tendency of the ethics of justifiable feticide which I have sketched here runs directly contrary to the tide of practice, not only in Britain but all over the world. The facts of the incidence of induced abortion invite only one conclusion: that abortion is now being more widely legalized and practised because that is what people want – an indication for medical intervention for the destruction of life unknown in our ethics before. Formal respect is paid to the conscience of doctors and nurses who decline to participate: the English Act of 1967 has a specific conscience clause in it. But objectors are constantly under all sorts of pressures to conform, including that of being questioned at interview, on application for appointments or consultancies, upon willingness to perform abortions. Indeed, the Abortion Law Reform Association (ALRA) in its formal evidence to the (Lane) Committee of Enquiry into the working of the Act, actually made the recommendation:

> Where there is only one gynaecological consultant serving an area, or where none is doing abortions, assurance should be sought before making any new appointment that the applicant is willing to perform abortions.

In comment on its own recommendation ALRA added:

> It may seem hard for an applicant to be turned down solely on account of his refusal to perform abortions, but we maintain that the sacrifice must be his and no one else's, least of all the women who do not share his beliefs.

Scant respect is paid here either to professional discretion or to the intentions of the Act.

One long-standing convention is being swept away. Those who regret its passing have a clear moral duty. It is to strive with concerted might to create conditions for its return – or for its replacement with something better. I have indicated areas of scientific, medical and technological advance which reduce maternal risks in pregnancy, increase the possibilities of pre-natal diagnosis and even of pre-natal repair, and make life more comfortable, more full of human possibility, for the handicapped child if born. There is a duty to further these advances, and to make their benefits known, as there is a duty, of course, to make reliable and acceptable means of contraception universally available. There is, above all, a duty to heighten these peculiarly human responses of acceptance, respect for persons, intelligent and loving care which assure to the handicapped and the disadvantaged a place in that complex of moral and emotional community which we call humanity. These are the essential moral conditions for any principled or Christian opposition to the 'liberalizing' of the laws governing abortion: without them, opposition has no credibility, no moral base.[22]

II

It is not a far step from the problem of abortion to that of 'euthanasia', the deliberate termination of life by medical intervention. The two are logically connected, in that both presuppose the same right over life; and both are demanded in terms of 'liberalization' of the law. Their ethics may be comparably discussed, too, if we give to euthanasia some precise terms cognate with *feticide* and linked, of course, to *homicide* and *suicide*: *infanticide* for the killing of infants, perhaps because born with gross handicap; *senicide* for the killing of the aged; *dementicide* or *amenticide* for the killing of those whom we judge mentally incompetent to live. With a terminology like this we can discuss what it is proposed that we should actually do; it is more manageable than words like 'the painless inducement of death' with which euthanasia was defined in Lord Raglan's Voluntary Euthanasia Bill, the last to come before the English Parliament, in 1969.

The plea that doctors be authorized to kill – or to instruct nurses to kill on their behalf[23] – is commonly advanced in preference to three other courses. The first is living or dying 'in agony'. The second is 'having a useless life (or a vegetable existence) artificially prolonged'. The third is 'the lethal terminal dose' already administered, it is said, under the guise of relieving pain. All of these are over-simplifications or mis-statements of situations misunderstood.

Let it be granted that death comes to some in great pain, not only in emergencies but also where terminal care is still below the best. But the campaign for euthanasia is not mounted in regions where medicine is undeveloped. It is mounted where doctors and nurses have at their disposal a wide range of analgesic drugs which, selectively used, can and do ease the pain of death even in illnesses of themselves most painful; where more and more training is given, as at St Christopher's Hospice in South London, and at other pioneer centres, in the art of assuring to patients a good death, whether in hospital or at home. To kill the patient is not the only alternative to pain: there is a better way, namely to assuage the pain and make this solace more widely available. Let it be granted, too, that there are rare and extreme situations, for instance when in war men are trapped, unaided, isolated and alone, about which no moralist, from the comfort of his chair, would condemn the bullet fired as mercy's sole available resort. But the ethics of an extreme emergency situation are one; the ethics of normal professional care are another. We teach policemen on motorway patrols first aid; we do not teach them to kill motorists who are trapped.

What is meant, next, by 'the artificial prolongation of life?' It is true that in intensive care units patients whose vital functions have collapsed are given artificial support by machines. These are employed as temporary aids, either while remedial attempts are made, or until it can be discovered whether the organism, unsupported, is capable of spontaneous function or not. When hope of recovery is gone, the machine is switched off, the artificial support is removed. The notion of patients continuing endlessly wired up to machines is fictitious. The comatose or decerebrate person, crudely miscalled in polemical debate a 'vegetable', is in another case. His spontaneous vital functions continue, because the lower centres of the brain which control them are the only part of it unharmed; the cerebral cortex, which enables rational self-consciousness, is destroyed. He is not 'kept alive'; he lives. And while he lives, he is entitled to elementary human care, that is, nursing care, simply to be fed, turned, kept clean. Whether an attack of pneumonia, say, should be countered with active therapy, like an antibiotic, is another question: appropriate management might rather be to let the body fight its own battle, win or lose – there is no obligation, in such a case, to administer a particular remedy. Or who are the others said to be 'officiously kept alive'? They are the old, the senile, the mentally handicapped of every age. One or two speakers in the House of Lords, debating Lord Raglan's Bill, wanted to have them killed: Lord Ailwyn, for instance, could speak of

> the crying need to offer these poor creatures the one remedy one felt in one's bones that they might accept gratefully and thankfully grasp, ... this boon, this milk of human kindness, ... to be wafted painlessly into the life to come.[24]

Why? All they claim from us, and about all they are given, is the basic human claim, to shelter, warmth, food, elementary medical and nursing care, and a little companionship. They 'suffer' far less than the spectator suffers, who comes to assess their claim to life. And what of the voluntary element in voluntary euthanasia if *these* are candidates for clinically administered death? If their condition were but half as pathetic as it is said to be, they would be incapable of giving valid consent.

Children, severely handicapped from birth, are also on the list; especially babies born with myelomeningocele, or spina bifida. The ethics of appropriate care for these have been vigorously debated within a medical unit in Sheffield which has specialized in their treatment for a long period.[25] For ten years a team accepted every child brought to it, giving it the most energetic treatment possible in an effort to lessen handicap. The result was, in some cases, to prolong and intensify suffering into the years of greater awareness and sensitivity, as each intervention created the need of yet another later on. The policy of energetic treatment for all had to be changed to one of selection: treatment would be determined by the clinical prognosis of the future degree of handicap. This did not mean that some children would be left to suffer untreated, still less that they would be selected to be killed. Immediate repair is possible, and is given; nursing care is given, and all that can be done is done to lessen suffering – but nothing to prevent the release of death. This is appropriate management – neither killing, nor arrogantly keeping alive. It requires fine clinical judgment; but this is of the essence of medical care.

Thirdly, do doctors 'kill' already, with 'the lethal terminal dose'? To relieve the pains of death is undoubtedly proper medical treatment. A drug given to control pain may either prolong life a little, by lessening anguish and therefore strain, or it may induce a pulmonary condition which may shorten life. The giving of that drug plays no part in the legal causation of death, and is *not* the moral equivalent of 'euthanasia', of killing the patient deliberately. (Something quicker than an analgesic drug would be used for that, anyway.) The drug is given and directly intended for the relief of pain; the death of the patient follows (if it follows) as an unavoidable, secondary effect of that action – foreseeable indeed, but not directly intended – no less drastic remedy being available. This 'principle of double effect' is not popular among philosophers, chiefly, perhaps, because it can lend itself to specious abuse. But it is a principle with which we have to live in a world where absolute and unmingled good is not at our command. Euthanasia, or clinical homicide upon request, as it should properly be called, stands on a different moral footing: the act which kills the patient is intended and directed to that end and no other.

This preliminary exercise in clarification is necessary before the issue of euthanasia can be fairly faced. The question now before us is: would the licensing of a doctor or nurse to kill their patients give more or less protection to those basic interests in life which our moral conventions exist to protect?

Interests are not the same as wishes.[26] A patient may wish to die. It is a doctor's business to know why he wishes to die, and to serve the patient's interests by going to the root of the wish. To a clinical psychiatrist, the human instinct to live is so basic that a wish to die *must* be a sign of disorder, of pathological depression – a condition to be treated, if possible, and cured. The very possibility of signing, in advance, a form of consent to being killed at some future date would seriously invade the interest of aging, dependent people in the trust and security on which their enjoyment of life rests. In the ambivalence between wanting to live and 'hating to be a nuisance', any gesture of impatience from those looking after them could be misread as a signal, 'They want me out of the way: they want me to sign the form.' Crippling insecurity would result. These supporting relatives have interests. One interest is in being protected from the random – or even settled – wish, sometimes, to be free from the burden of a very trying charge. They too are ambivalent in their feelings; and the purpose of a convention, backed if necessary by law, is to act as a protective regulator. Other relatives, too, may have interests: they will have material interests, when property or inheritance is at stake, in the death of the patient, or perhaps in his staying alive beyond a given date, or in his freedom of decision in relation to his will. The defence of these interests is bound to generate suspicion, if ever it became possible for the patient to declare his wish to be killed, and for his medical attendants to kill him. That suspicion would overflow on to the doctor or the nurse as well, if the time of a patient's death proved expensively inconvenient for someone with an interest. The doctor would have his form of consent, and would flourish it; but it would not protect him from the necessity of defending himself in the courts, if an action were brought against him. He might not, indeed, have acted upon the consent given – the patient might have died without his encouragement. But the very suspicion that he might have caused the death, which legalized euthanasia would create, would be enough to raise the risks of litigation.

These are particular interests at risk in euthanasia. There is also a common interest which, as members of society, we all share. It is in an essential public confidence that doctors and nurses are servants of our health and well-being and will in no circumstances become our executioners. We can discuss euthanasia with rational detachment in the lecture room or the club, in enjoyment of our health. But in sickness, when vitality is low, rationality is weakened; our biological instinct to survive, to protect ourselves, throws up fears and fantasies. At present the syringe, the tablet or the draught in the hand of the nurse spells comfort if not cure. But once legislation has created the possibility that these were instruments of death, confidence would have gone; rationality alone would not protect us from even groundless fear. There are exceptions, calm, steady men. But life cannot be organized on the supposition that every man is a

Socrates. We need, as we now have, a complex of expectations, conventions, rituals, sanctions professional and legal, to maintain our interest in a basic social confidence that life is precious and is normally to be protected. We are not without the instinct with which birds and animals defend life; but those instincts are weakened in us. We support them in these other, rational, typically human, ways. They protect, not simply the lives of men but also the humanity of man. This is why we should not ask our doctors to put us or our kind to death.[27]

NOTES

1. *International Planned Parenthood Federation News* III.7, Supplement, July 1972.

2. Press Release, 14 April 1973, to accompany publication of its *Client Statistics for 1971*, British Pregnancy Advisory Service, Birmingham 1973.

3. In 1971 the charitable organizations arranged about 22,000 abortions, leaving to the commercial sector about 21,000 resident applicants; the commercial sector became increasingly reliant upon foreign women – 30,000 in 1971.

4. Op. cit., Table 1. Women counselled, 16,244; certificates refused, 156; certificates signed, 16,088.

5. *Nobis vero homicidio semel interdicto etiam conceptum in utero dum adhuc sanguis in hominem delibatur dissolvere non licet. Homicidii festinatio est prohibere nasci; nec refert natam quis eripiat animam an nascentem disturbat: homo est et qui est futurus; etiam fructus omnis jam in semine est.* Tertullian, *Apol.* 9.8.

6. See J. T. Noonan, Jr, *Contraception: A History of its Treatment by the Catholic Theologians and Canonists*, Harvard University Press and Oxford University Press 1965, pp. 86ff.; J. T. Noonan, Jr, ed. *The Morality of Abortion: Legal and Historical Perspectives*, Harvard University Press 1970.

7. *Watt* v *Rama* (1972) VR 353, *The Times*, 10 January 1973.

8. See A. J. Quinn and J. A. Griffin, 'The Rights of the Unborn', *The Jurist*, 1971.4, pp. 577-613. Contrast the ruling of the US Supreme Court in *Roe* v *Wade*, US 35 L Ed 2d 147, 93 S Ct, 1973, that the right to privacy under the Fourteenth Amendment grants a woman the right to decide whether or not to abort her child during the first tremester.

9. The Law Commission, London, *Injuries to Unborn Children*; Published Working Paper No. 47, 1973.

10. Quinn and Griffin, p. 586.

11. *Commentaries*, 4th edn, 1770, i. p. 129.

12. Ibid., pp. 581f., 603.

13. *The Use of Fetuses and Fetal Material for Research:* The Report

of an Advisory Group to the Department of Health and Social Security, HMSO 1972, paras. 26, 28, 35, and the Recommended Code of Practice, p. 12. This is discussed by R. W. Smithells et al., 'Research Investigation and the Fetus', *British Medical Journal*, 26 May 1973, in a series on 'New Horizons in Medical Ethics'.

14. J. Delmaille, in *Dictionnaire de Droit Canonique*, ed. by R. Naz, 1935, s. v. 'Avortement'. Considered in *Abortion: An Ethical Discussion*, Church Information Office 1065.

15. Gregory of Nyssa, *Adversus Macedonianos*, trans. from Library of Nicene and Post-Nicene Fathers, ser. 2, vol. V, ed. H. Wace and P. Schaff, Oxford and New York 1893, p. 320. Greek: *to atelesphorēton embruon alla dunamenon eiper etelesphorēthē eis anthrōpou genesin proelthein* (*Gregorii Nysseni Opera Dogmatica Minora*, 1, ed. F. Mueller, Brill, Leiden 1958, p. 101).

16. *The Irish Penitentials*, ed. Ludwig Bieler; Scriptores Latini Hiberniae, Dublin 1963, p. 229; cf. p. 161.

17. See *Abortion: An Ethical Discussion*, and R. F. R. Anderson, *Abortion: The Personal Dilemma*, Paternoster Press 1972.

18. *The Registrar-General's Statistical Review of England and Wales for the Year 1971*; Part I, Medical Tables, HMSO, published 8 March 1973.

19. *Report on Confidential Enquiries into Maternal Deaths in England and Wales 1967-1969*, HMSO, published 17 Aug. 1972.

20. *Abortion: An Ethical Discussion*, p. 67.

21. The then Bishop of Durham, the Rt Revd I. T. Ramsey. He justified his affirmative vote with a statement that, although in its final form the Bill was not what he would have wished, its rejection would have created a worse situation. Documentation is to be found in *Hansard*, H. of L., 19 July and 3 and 23 Oct. 1967, and in a letter from the Bishop to *The Times*.

22. Cf. 'A New Catholic Strategy on Abortion', *The Month*, London, CCXXXIV, 1269, May 1973, pp. 163ff.

23. Lord Raglan's Bill, S. 4 (2). Lord Raglan has subsequently ceased his advocacy of euthanasia. See *The Problem of Euthanasia*, Contact (Pastoral) Ltd, Edinburgh, Supplement to *Contact*, Summer 1972.

24. Hansard. H. of L., vol. 300, no. 50, 25 March 1969, coll. 1186f.

25. J. Lorber, 'Results of Treatment of Myelomeningocele', *Developmental Care and Child Neurology*, 1971, xiii, 3, pp. 279-303; B. M. Freeston, 'An Enquiry into the Effect of a Spina Bifida Child on Family Life', ibid, xiii. 4, pp. 456-61; J. H. Walker et al., 'Spina Bifida and the Parents', ibid., pp. 462-76; R. B. Zachary, 'Ethical and Social Aspects of Treatment of Spina Bifida', *The Lancet*, 3 Aug. 1968, pp. 274-6; H. B. Eckstein et al., 'Severely Malformed Children', *British Medical Journal*, 5 May 1973, in a series on 'New Horizons in Medical Ethics'; see also *The Times*, 26 Oct. 1973.

26. See a discussion between two philosophers, B. G. Mitchell and R. M. Hare, in *Personality and Science*, ed. I. T. Ramsey and Ruth Porter, Churchill Livingstone 1971, ch. 12.

27. Another treatment of euthanasia, more favourable than this one, is to be found in P. R. Baelz, 'Voluntary Euthanasia: Some Theological Reflections', *Theology* LXXV, 1972, p. 238. See also Hugh Trowell, *The Unfinished Debate on Euthanasia*, SCM Press 1973.

6

Conventions in Restraint of Power

A teacher of moral theology in a university today is, if he may take a phrase from one of the older versions of the Bible, a very lucky fellow. He is stretched continually between radicalism and reality, and that is both good for him and agreeable. He lives with students – and by living is meant engaging with them, in tutorial and seminar discussion – among whom many bring, in all good faith, radical or idealist solutions to the world's most intractable problems. They have, of course, a language for this ready to hand in the Gospels. World poverty could be abolished *if* the rich, nations, churches and individuals, simply sold all that they had and gave to the poor. Wars would not occur *if* all men lived peaceably with one another as Jesus said they should. The endless entail of violence bred of violence would be broken *if* men turned the other cheek, following the non-violent way of Jesus who, 'when he was reviled, reviled not again; when he suffered, he threatened not'. There would be no racial discrimination *if* we saw in all men 'the brother for whom Christ died'; no discrimination against women *if* we realized that in Christ Jesus 'there can be no male and female' – though it is odd to observe that it is the word of St Paul, not of Jesus, which is relied on here.[1] These are the major premises from which sincere Christians make their first moves into the discussion of social ethics. These, too, give them common ground, or the appearance of it, with radicals of another sort who also hate the injustices, tyrannies and inequalities of this present world, and are determined to overthrow the 'structures' which contain them; and that common ground can be a source both of strength and of embarrassment. This is the company which the moralist, lucky man, can keep.

He moves also in other company, among realists. He has to

show but a flicker of intelligent interest in men's real problems
to be invited to sit among bankers and company directors while
they hammer out the practical demands of justice in relation
to their actual business responsibilities; or among civil servants,
diplomatists and ministers of the Crown charged with the day-
to-day negotiations on arms control and disarmament; or among
soldiers, policemen and journalists balancing the claims of
security against the defence of individual liberty while they are
literally targets for the terrorist's bomb or bullet. In other
words, the pursuit of a relevant ethics which takes him out of
the library and classroom and into the company of medical
scientists and practitioners for some of his tasks, takes him out
also among men wielding political and economic power for
others. This I called being stretched between radicalism and
reality.

Both words, of course, being now incapable of precise use, are
imprecisely used. The Christian theologian is committed to the
belief that 'reality' is the life which Jesus embodied and taught,
not that caricature of life which is the embodiment of all our
troubles. Christian 'radicalism', therefore, is a return to this
'reality'; it is improper to set these words in contrast. To pursue
that point would be to work again the major question, touched
on earlier in these lectures, of the relation between the ethics
or first-order principles of the Kingdom of God and the ethics
or second-order rules necessary for the government of human
society in the kingdoms of this world. For my present purpose
I have to point to that repeated *if* in the radicalists' statements
as the logical flaw in their attempt to establish a workable ethics.
Men, in fact, do *not* sell all that they have and give to the poor
– there would be economic chaos if they did; they do *not* live
peaceably with one another; they do *not*, invariably, turn the
other cheek in personal relations, and in political and international relations they would sometimes consider it immoral to
do so. They do not live as Jesus did; and, moreover, they cannot.
They live with disordered natures in a disordered world. Their
major ethical task, therefore, is the control of power: to create
and maintain a fabric of order within which men may enjoy the
utmost freedom to pursue the good life, to practise the highest
virtues, forgiving one another when they fail. The words of
Jesus were not directed towards this problem, partly because he

had another task, partly because he lived within a community, founded upon law, which took all this for granted. The practical uselessness of Christian radicalism in the short term, as Michael Howard has pointed out,[2] stems from its ignoring the duties attending the use of power for the sake of the fabric of order; though in the longer term, as Dr Geoffrey Nuttall has argued from Quaker history,[3] and as the present sacrificial intrusion of local Christians into politics in Southern Africa and both Americas daily shows, Christian radicalism, accompanied by suffering, is necessary for the unceasing task of creating a more just and merciful social order.

The artifice of ethics, therefore, has both its short-term and its long-term ends: in the short term, the fashioning of ethical tools for the task of dealing with the disorders that are – including, for example, rules to govern the conduct of war while wars are waged; in the long term, the enlivening of conscience, the heightening of moral sensitivity, and the putting of higher insights into human keeping in the form of institutions, political, social, economic, conventional to enable the world to live more brotherly and humanly than it lives now. These tasks are not separate: it is my belief that in our actual pursuit of conventions to deal with our present problems of power we can create the conditions of trust without which no longer-term advance can be made. The essence of the convention is mutual trust.

I

Throughout the time when these lectures were being written, the daily newspapers were reporting relevant contests: the attempt, led by Australia and New Zealand, to deter the French Government from nuclear tests in the Pacific area; the determination, first of the American press, and then of a Federal Grand Jury and a Senate Committee, to uncover irregularities connected with President Nixon's re-election campaign (telephone tapping, theft of documents, unaccounted contributions to political funds); and the resort to the Law Courts, and to an inspection by the Department of Trade and Industry, to regulate the management of the Lonrho trading group.[4] Common to all three contests is the attempt by society to protect itself against grave threats to its security, environmental, political and economic. It is the function of law, in a civilized community, to give that protection, but here law fails conspicuously to give it. The French Government refuses to recognize the competence of the International Court of Justice to grant the injunctions sought against the tests by the Australian and New Zealand Governments;[5] and even when the Court has granted the injunctions, it has no power to enforce its judgment. Without power under ethical control, justice cannot be done. In the American affair, the major object of enquiry is not the criminal conduct of individuals but the power of the political administration to impede or override the processes of justice and to secure immunity for itself from the rule of law. In the Lonrho case it must be assumed, until the contrary is proved, that the directors whose activities have caused such concern acted within the law contained in the Companies Acts and the laws governing taxation and exchange control. All commercial experience, however, goes to confirm a truth long established in moral theology and experience, that in a straight conflict between self-interest and law, self-interest will win: human ingenuity will always find loopholes in the law, or bend its terms to personal advantage. We are back with Lord Devlin's doctrine, expounded in the first of these lectures, that without the intervention of conscience, law cannot govern: there must be a moral basis of trust.

So the moralist observes in the daily newspaper, in the circulation of discussion documents and drafts, the search for conventions in restraint of power. Fears of the political misuse of neuro-surgery or 'psycho-surgery' in the USA to 'brain-wash' dissidents, or to remove their disruptive potential, are at present arousing controversy about control.[6] Clearly, Government must not be the controller, since it could be itself the instigator of abuse. But neither may every practitioner be left free to do what he likes: there must be some other guardian of the liberties of such persons as the inmates of penal and other institutions who are at risk as subjects for experiment precisely because of their limited power of refusal, or through an exploitation of their yearning to be free. These matters have exercised psychiatrists, philosophers, lawyers and moralists in England for several years.[7] To counter the threat to privacy and personal interest involved in the storage of information in the computer, the British Computer Society has produced, after three and a

half years of discussion, a voluntary *Code of Good Practice*.[8] The Estate Agents Council has issued a code of conduct for its members, enforceable by suspension, reprimand or removal from the register.[9]

The Confederation of British Industry has had a working party engaged in drawing up a code of practice for the corporate conduct of public companies. It produced first an interim report,[10] setting out the areas in which power may be exercised irresponsibly, and in which therefore it must be controlled; so it covered the supervisory responsibility of shareholders, the merits and demerits of 'two-tier' or 'supervisory' boards on the German model, the proper regulation of take-overs, mergers and multi-national corporations, and the representation of the interests of employees and of consumers in the management. Its aim was to set a voluntary standard of behaviour above the minimum required by law; an enabling clause would be inserted in the Memorandum of Association, and there would be a review panel to oversee the working of the code; but no sanction other than that of public opinion formed, presumably, by comment in the financial press. The final report, *The Responsibilities of the British Company*, published in September 1973, took account of a Government White Paper on Company Law Reform (Cmnd 5391) anticipating a new legal structure in which reprehensible commercial behaviour would be controlled. The CBI, therefore, declined for itself responsibility for promulgating or enforcing a code, and contented itself with the enunciation of Principles of Corporate Conduct, with detailed application to the activities of the board room. The Christian Association of Business Executives has gone further. Drawing on preliminary surveys of British business men's behaviour and ethical attitudes,[11] it has published a draft code, with proposals for enforcement. Also in the autumn of 1973 the Institute of Directors published *Guidelines for Directors*, 'to set before directors the standards of behaviour followed in well-conducted companies', with the clear implication that they ought to be followed in others; and the Institute of Marketing promulgated a *Code of Practice* to govern the professional conduct of its members, with a disciplinary procedure and with expulsion as the final sanction for offenders. The initiatives in these measures come from business men themselves; they attach moralists and lawyers to themselves only for the necessary clarification of the moral and legal issues involved.[12]

II

I have given examples of efforts to contain power in the normal circumstances of modern living. But what of war, when normality is abandoned in the resort to force, and power seeks only to maximize itself with no other intent than to destroy the enemy power: is moral reasoning then also at an end? Is there any place for convention in restraint of war? I wish to argue that there is. I wish to combat that moral resignation or despair which sees modern war as so horrible and destructive that moral considerations can have no place in it. I wish to awaken or confirm an intelligent and committed interest in that patient work of diplomacy which seeks, year in year out, to lessen the hazards of war and so to increase the likelihood of the survival of our race and civilization.

Idealist critics might say at once that this is no proper task for a Christian theologian. His task, they might argue, is straightforward: he should take up the mantle of Christian prophecy, denounce war unconditionally as evil, and call upon the nations to renounce the use of force – by common consent if possible, or, if not, by his own nation alone as a forcible demonstration for the truth and as a move towards universal peace. I am not able to perform that task, for reasons indicated when I referred to the teaching of Jesus and the context of the preservation of order. I must draw attention also to a supposition on which it would rest. The proposal that war could be renounced by common consent rests on a supposition that nations can be brought to a common consent, and that there is sufficient good faith for an agreement, even to renounce war, to be trusted. Without this degree of mutual trust no practical consequences would flow from the declared renunciation: no nation would begin to disarm, or to renounce a thermo-nuclear capability, unless it could feel confident that others would do the same. The more radical proposal, to renounce war unilaterally, must have a similar act of faith built into it. It may, of course, be intended as an heroic witness to the truth, come what may: this nation will not fight, it would declare, even though its total

destruction or domination by an aggressor might follow. This
would be an extreme view, and the only one, I think, which
could claim any support or parallel from the death of Jesus on
the cross: nowhere can we derive from the gospel any doctrine
of non-resistance *with survival*; there is no warrant there for
non-resistance as a political weapon. The less extreme view
would be that such an act of renunciation, even by one power
alone, is necessary to break the circle of mutual fear and suspicion which holds all nations to arms: other nations would
follow, and so there would be a general move towards peace. But
this view also presupposes trust – faith in the moral responsive-
ness of other nations and in the consistency of their policies.
The view of the unconditional pacifist, therefore (except in its
extreme form, that it is better for the nation to be destroyed
than to fight) presupposes trust; the capacity in nations to
respond to a pacific overture; the possibility of sufficient agreement among nations to withhold or renounce some exercise
of military power in their common interest. It is precisely on this
capacity for mutual trust, or dependability, that I wish to build
my argument for conventions in restraint of war. Even those
who, on Christian grounds, might consider my attempt to be no
more than an unworthy compromise with politics, must allow
that my prescription stands on the same footing as theirs,
namely a capacity for mutual trust or dependability between
nations. (This trust has, of course, a theological foundation in
the capacity of man made in God's image to reflect the faithfulness of God; but that is another story.)

Nations, and national sovereignties, are indeed an anachron-
ism – though they have taken a new and vigorous lease of life
in peoples newly independent, while older nations tend to cur-
tail their sovereignty in regional association, as in the European
Economic Community. The world needs a new political organization which will enable it to develop a unity which fully
respects diversity, political, economic, social, cultural, religious.[13]
But every step in this direction demands trust, without which
nations will not lower the barriers which they erect one against
the other. Until an international political community is created
and both trusted and invested with adequate power, we are left
with the fact of national states, each armed with power; and

therefore with the task of regulating their use of power to the common advantage.

Realists might now counter my argument with a denial that this common ground exists: there is no trust, they might say; no nation can be depended on to abate its use of force when its interests are threatened, or even when a chance to further its own power occurs; the only security lies in possessing greater power, and in being prepared to use it to the limit of necessity; we deal, not in morals, but in politics, and politics is simply the application of power. But this argument is over-moralistic; it limits the notion of trust to an altruistic trust, one without self-interest. The moralist is less naïve. In his understanding of men he knows that while he must always appeal to altruism, he must also reckon with self-interest. The political philosopher, in the high tradition, is no different. The trust, the dependability, on which I rely is one in which is entrenched legitimate and ordinate self-interest, that of the maxim, 'Do to others as you would they should do to you', and of its opposite, 'Do not do to others what you would not wish them to do to you'. Politics is to do with survival; it is in our common interest to survive.[14]

My assumptions are, therefore, that war is not so much a tragic necessity as a tragic fact in the world; that there are legitimate uses of armed force in the preservation of a people against external attack or internal disruption; that the whole concept of legitimacy in the use of force is one which can and must be made the object of agreement between nations; that there is sufficient capacity for trust or dependability between them for this agreement to be possible; and that capacity grows with the attempt. The assumptions are not new. For centuries they were embodied in the tradition of 'the just war'. In recent times they have been the ground of international law and conventions which mark steps in agreement between nations,[15] even though they have been broken.

The tradition did not originate with Christianity; it is older. The Christian tradition took it over from Greek and Roman sources. It has done more to relieve the sufferings of mankind than the crude notions of the holy war or crusade and the war of vengeance or of extermination which were, in less enlightened centuries, wrested from the more primitive elements in the Bible. It began in Greece with some simple propositions about the *jus ad bellum*, the cause for which a city might justly go to war: war should be a last resort only after mediation had failed; war should be undertaken only for the vindication of justice and to restore a lasting peace. Thence it moved on to the *jus in bello*, the just conduct of a war once it had begun: war should be so conducted as not to preclude this lasting peace; violence should be limited to the minimum necessary to gain satisfaction from the enemy; there should be no deliberate burning of houses, scorching of the earth, or outrage to humanity or destruction of social order; the conquered, if Greeks, were not to be exterminated or enslaved. These were typical of attempts made to limit the damage of war among civilized Greek city-states, among groups between whom faith and agreement were possible; the barbarians were excluded from the provisions precisely because such faith and dependability could not be assumed. Later the tradition was developed, codified, defined and extended, first by the Romans, then by Christian thinkers, St Augustine, St Thomas Aquinas, Vitoria, Calvin, Suarez. It passed into modern times in the writings of Grotius, who reinterpreted it in the categories of law. Its principles may be seen, by the discerning eye, in the language of modern Roman Catholic statements, notably in the papal encyclical *Pacem in Terris* (1963) and in *Gaudium et Spes*, the Pastoral Constitution of the Second Vatican Council on The Church and the Modern World (1965). It underlies and controls the thought of Professor Paul Ramsey, a major contributor to contemporary discussion of the ethics of war. Above all, it is the very ground of existing international law and conventions, stemming from the Hague and Geneva, in which nations have striven 'to reconcile the interests of humanity with the demands of military necessity'. It is even written into the 'yellow card' carried by British troops to regulate their action against terrorists in Ulster.[16] This lecture comes, then, out of a living tradition linking us with men over two and a half thousand years who have devised conventions for the restraint of military power.

This is not the place to investigate all the principles which have been incorporated, from time to time, in that tradition, nor their continuing degrees of relevance in a changed world. The doctrine, for instance, that war might properly be undertaken only at the command of a proper sovereign authority would put into question all unilateral action by today's sovereign states until there emerged an accepted world authority capable of exercising that command. The putting of forces at the disposal of the United Nations Security Council, in accordance with Article 39 of the UN Charter, is a tentative step in that direction. Widespread (if *bona fide*) condemnation of unilateral action when it happens, e.g., in the Anglo-French attack at Suez, or in the hostilities between Egypt and Israel, point the same way. Many of today's wars, too, are insurgency wars, waged *against* constituted authority; it would be retrogressive to deny insurgent forces, on that ground, the protection of other just war principles, or to fail to require their own compliance with them. They are, in international law, granted limited belligerent rights. Similarly, the rule that before embarking on war or revolution there must be a reasonable prospect of success – a rule that encouraged prolonged and barbarous cruelty when it was turned into a requirement of success in order to justify the initial act of war – would now involve intricate and hazardous calculations of the short-term or long-term probability, not only of victory, but also of capacity to establish a régime more just than the one overthrown. Many were the miscalculations over the Biafran attempt to secede from Nigeria, and few would have predicted the defeat of the USA in Vietnam. Yet the rule is as relevant to the timing of a revolution against a tyrannous government today as it was to the abortive plot against Hitler.[17]

There are, however, two fundamental principles in the doctrine which govern practical decisions still today, and which are entrenched in the law and conventions, those already established and those now being formed. These are the principles of proportion and discrimination. Proportion has a part in the ethics of war not unlike its part in the ethics of medicine. 'There must be a reasonable proportion between the injury caused by any use of force and the good effected or the graver ill prevented.'[18] The principle forms part of the *jus ad bellum*: 'The good to be attained by war must be reasonably supposed to be greater than the certain evils, material and spiritual, which war entails.' The justice of rebellion, also, 'must be in proportion to the injustice of the government.... It is only if the coercion [exercised by government] is out of all proportion to the needs of government, and taking into account also external threats, that violent revolution is justified.'[19] The balance has to be weighed, therefore, between the claims of order and of justice. The devastation inherent in modern war, and increasingly in contemporary insurgency and revolution, is such that oppressed populations may have to suffer injustice rather than risk the extended destruction of order entailed in a resort to force: even a fishing dispute (as in 1972-3 between England and Iceland) or a revolution, as in Vietnam, may lead to intervention by other powers and so to international war, perhaps to nuclear war. It was this consideration of proportion which excluded armed intervention after the Russian invasions of Hungary and Czechoslovakia and the Rhodesian unilateral declaration of independence.

Proportion is also part of the *jus in bello*. It expresses itself in the rule of minimum necessary force. 'Only so much violence may be used as is necessary: in the case of defence, only so much as is necessary to repel the violence of the aggressor.'[20] (This is, incidentally, an elementary rule in English police discipline.) The means taken, both strategic and tactical, must be proportionate to the end to be achieved, and the force or destruction employed must not go beyond necessity, nor be such as to make a just settlement the more difficult to achieve. The principle, as applied, for instance, in the Geneva Conventions codified in 1949, stands to protect not only civilians but also combatant soldiers: since the object of an action against a combatant is not necessarily to destroy him but is primarily to disable him from further attack, the action must be proportionate to that end; once he ceases to be a potential attacker, by reason of capture, surrender or disablement, he becomes entitled to humane treatment and protection.

With proportion goes the principle of discrimination, which distinguishes between combatant and non-combatant, and forbids a *direct* attack on persons taking no active part in the hostilities – another attempt to apply the rule of protection for 'innocent' life. The principle was asserted in the Pastoral Constitution on the Church in the Modern World of Vatican II:

> Any act of war aimed indiscriminately at the destruction of entire cities or of extensive areas along with their population is a crime against God and man himself. It merits unequivocal and unhesitating condemnation.[21]

The classification of protected persons has varied in different epochs, and it is vigorously debated now when the whole active population is mobilized for war, and not only its armed forces and munitions workers; and when, in insurgency warfare, a peasant by day can become a guerrilla fighter by night.[22] But the principle is too valuable to be abandoned, despite the difficulty of its application. Without it there would be no ground on which to condemn such outrages as those disclosed in the My Lai trials, and no restraint laid upon soldiers in hot pursuit of terrorists in areas congested with non-combatant (though perhaps sympathetic and even participant) women and children. The principle does not claim to shield non-combatants absolutely from indirect or collateral harm, from hurt accidentally sustained in an attack on a legitimate military target – but only from *direct* attack, intended for their hurt. Acceptance of the principle obliges governments to keep military installations away from concentrations of civilian population, or to provide adequately for their protection. In insurgency situations, as in Ulster, it requires a high standard of military discipline, and reliable means of establishing the facts when civilians become casualties during exchanges of fire. It is significant that when this happens the insurgents, who think nothing of indiscriminate murder by means of bombs and booby traps in bars and cars, use civilian deaths as propaganda material against their military and political opponents; this would not be possible unless there were a conscience against indiscriminate attack to which they can appeal.[23]

The relevance of these principles to the just war traditions is frequently questioned. Before the objections are examined, a simple example may be given of their place, in combination, in a document in daily use, the 'yellow card' embodying 'Instructions by the Director of Operations for Opening Fire in Northern Ireland', as issued in November 1971.

GENERAL RULES

2. Never use more force than the minimum necessary to enable you to carry out your duties.

3. Always first try to handle the situation by other means than by opening fire. If you have to fire:
   (*a*) Fire only aimed shots.

(*b*) Do not fire more rounds than are absolutely necessary to achieve your aim.

[Proportion]

You may fire after due warning

8. Against a person carrying what you can positively identify as a firearm, but only if you have reason to think that he is about to use it for offensive purposes ...

9. Against a person throwing a petrol bomb ...

10. Against a person attacking or destroying property or stealing firearms or explosives, if his action is likely to endanger life...

19. At a road block/check you will NOT fire on a vehicle simply because it refused to stop....

[Discrimination]

But now it is time to consider two grounds on which my argument is open to grave attack. The first is, the frequency and regularity with which these principles are disregarded in actual war. Both sides disregarded them in the bombing of cities in the second world war, and the war was ended by the most indiscriminate and unproportioned act of all, the use of atomic bombs on Hiroshima and Nagasaki. Both sides violated them again in the Vietnam war, the Vietcong in its terrorist attacks on towns and villages, the Americans in their obliteration bombing, use of napalm, and the acknowledged crime of the massacre of village women and children, the South Vietnamese in the publicized shooting of prisoners. The facts are not in dispute. But the argument is not thereby overthrown. We do not repeal our laws against murder because men murder; we do not abandon our conventions in favour of chastity or truth because men are unchaste or untruthful. It is precisely the work of civilized men – part of the artifice of ethics – to re-assert the principle, and to strive to re-establish its acceptance, whenever it is broken.

The second ground of attack on my argument is more serious. It is that modern weapons of war make discrimination impossible, and that, however proportionate the first military measures may be to the end to be achieved, escalation is inevitable until proportion and discrimination alike are blown to the winds in an all-out thermo-nuclear exchange. Indeed, the need for one nuclear-armed nation to strike first against another might eliminate even the gradualness of escalation; the war would end virtually in its beginning. The threat lies also in chemical and bacteriological warfare, the first already experienced, the second so far unused (so far as we know) in war. How can I rescue my thesis from an objection so strong as this?

I reply that the argument is circular, taking its conclusion as a premiss. The threat of destruction by thermo-nuclear or bacteriological weapons cannot be denied; it might become inevitable if the very principle which I seek to maintain were abandoned – the principle of stated war aims to be pursued by limited and proportionate means – and replaced by the aim of total victory to be achieved regardless of means. Morally the objection is enervating: to abandon principles of control because of the threat of lack of control leading to unimaginable disaster, is to give way to despair. My case is precisely that it is only by securing attachment to the principles of control that the ultimate disaster can be avoided.

This is a different application of the just war principles from that of Paul Ramsey, who seeks (or, at least, sought when his book was published in 1968) to defend the thesis that even a thermo-nuclear war could be fought within the principles of proportion and discrimination. My thesis is that the principles are the ground on which international agreement must be founded to make a nuclear war impossible. Ramsey, especially in chapters 11, 13 and 15 of his book, *The Just War*, sets out a policy for the USA on the ground of discrimination: he would have his nation declare that it would never be the first to use thermo-nuclear weapons; secondly, that it would use them tactically only against forces crossing defined boundaries and only against military targets, but never *directly* against civilian populations. He would repudiate in advance all direct counter-city reprisals, believing not only that such acts are *mala in se* – evil in themselves – and that the distinction between killing and murder is to be maintained, even in war; but also that indiscriminate warfare cannot now achieve any good end, so that it is both wrong and foolish to commit such wrongs, or to threaten to do so, in order that good might come. The deterrent effect of a nuclear capacity would lie in the certainty of collateral or *indirect* damage to the enemy population arising inevitably from, though not intended by, direct nuclear attack on military targets. The casualty rate, of course, is estimated in millions. It would seem that logic here goes beyond moral sense: deaths by the million, foreseen and inevitable but not directly intended, are scarcely easier to contemplate than the same result achieved by direct attack: the context of both, in either case, is total devastation. Neither does the argument seem to be strengthened by the recent announcement from the Pentagon of the development of 'mini-nukes', miniature nuclear weapons which could be selected to inflict specific heat, or blast or radiation fall-out damage according to the target chosen. Leaving aside the discussion of technological feasibility – and considerable scepticism is expressed about this – its addition to the NATO armoury in Europe would be politically and morally disastrous: politically, because it would increase reliance on nuclear capability with a corresponding decline in readiness with conventional forces; morally because it would, in the guise of one more tactically deployable field-piece with an explosive power scarcely higher than that of conventional high explosive, obliterate the distinction between what is a nuclear weapon and what is not, and so ease the path to nuclear escalation from the moment of first use,[24] or even before.

Rather, then, than rely on ever more ingenuity in inventing means of nuclear annihilation, rather than lapse into moral despair at the thought that no rules would save us in the holocaust if it came, it is better to realize, first, that we have now lived for nearly thirty years since Nagasaki, with no nuclear war but with 'conventional' wars, somewhere or other, nearly all the time; and secondly that it is in our common interest to use the respite gained by the nuclear balance of power to assure that the nuclear holocaust never comes. Professor D. H. N. Johnson has stated the conclusion of my argument in one paragraph:

Even if chivalry be discounted in modern war, the assertion that the legal regulation of armed conflict is inconceivable involves proving the proposition that the contestants share no common values whatever, that they can afford totally to disregard public opinion at home as well as in neutral countries and that in the ruthless pursuit of military victory they are prepared to neglect altogether the situation that will confront them after the conclusion of hostilities. It is doubtful if these propositions are valid, and paradoxically today military necessity, which used to be the main problem in subjecting war to law, is now one of the strongest arguments in favour of regulation. For, however far military staffs of opposing belligerents are prepared to go to obtain their respective ends, they share a common interest in avoiding total annihilation.[25]

Despite the difficulties – and no one is more aware of them than the negotiators themselves – the signs are not discouraging. The major task is the promotion of confidence, trust: without this barriers arise. No agreement to limit the production or stock-piling of particular weapons is acceptable without means of verification; for large-scale nuclear explosions this can be done by remote seismic monitoring, with instruments of increasing sensitivity; silos and nuclear rocket emplacements are detectable by scanning from satellites; but the production and stocking of chemical weapons cannot be detected without on-site inspection; and this is precisely what an insecure, untrusting, nation, sensitive to 'espionage', cannot permit. This is the main hindrance to a Comprehensive Nuclear Test Ban and to a convention banning chemical weapons.

Nevertheless, there is ground for encouragement. There was progress, however slow, in the exploratory talks in Vienna in the spring of 1973 on mutual balanced force reduction in Europe. A more notable advance was begun in the signature and ratification of the Biological Weapons Convention accepted in the United Nations Assembly in the autumn of 1971. It was opened for signature on 10 April 1972, and by September it had already been signed by more than ninety countries, and ratified by six. Once ratified by twenty-two governments it will enter into force.[26] When chemical and biological weapons, their nature and the effects of their possible use, are examined as they were by an expert UN Committee,[27] it is clear that both sorts are to be condemned because they cannot be used discriminately or with controlled effect; and because the harm they would inflict, both on the course of the war and on its outcome in terms of the ends pursued, would be out of all proportion to any legitimate military or political aim. This is particularly true of biological weapons because of the many and uncontrollable variables attending their use – wind, temperature, humidity, nature of the terrain, and all forms of life inhabiting it.

The Convention therefore binds all parties never, in any circumstances, to develop, produce, stockpile or otherwise acquire biological weapons, to destroy existing stocks, and to consult and co-operate in achieving the purposes of the Convention. Alleged breaches are to be reported to the Security Council, and parties are to co-operate, again, in assisting states exposed to danger.

Article IX bound the parties to work together in good faith towards agreement on another convention, for the total prohibition of chemical weapons also. The Russians tabled a draft, modelled closely upon the biological weapons convention, on 28 March 1972, six days after the Americans had produced a 'Work Program' for consideration in the Conference of the UN Committee on Disarmament. The US paper pointed to the difficulties, chief among which is this: the use of biological agents or toxins for peaceful or prophylactic purposes is very limited, and the quantities involved are small; many ingredients in chemical weapons, by contrast, have extensive industrial and other peaceful uses, and the quantities involved are vast; some lethal agents, for instance, were developed as a by-product of research into insecticides, and some defoliants from research into crop improvement. Verification, therefore, monitoring and sealing are considered essential in any convention; otherwise no state will deprive itself of sufficient chemical warfare capability to retaliate in kind if attacked. (It is to be remembered that in the second world war both sides were fully equipped for chemical warfare; neither waged it, because of the certainty of reprisals.) Until there is trust, the threat of reprisals is a deterrent to use. Verification by on-site inspection is precisely what the Russians refuse to allow.

Progress is therefore slow; little was done at Geneva in the spring of 1973, except to involve all active members of the Conference except one in a resolution of support for keeping on to the main objective, a total ban on the production and possession of chemical weapons. The effort involved, however, is not wasted. Behind the rhetoric of the conference room, behind the drafts and counter-drafts, stands the work done in the corridors, more by the permanent civil servants and diplomatists than by the politicians, men whose business it is, by the patient searching for understanding and agreement, to bring all parties to the goal which all wish to attain, but to which none dares to go alone. Not for nothing were these bearers of the diplomatic burden singled out for encouragement and for prayer in the Second Vatican Council,[28] for they are the artificers of trust.

And trust is the artefact of ethics, the keystone of all institutions built to support and shelter the frail but precious moral judgments of mankind.

NOTES

1. I Cor. 8.11; Gal. 3.28; Col. 3.11.
2. Michael Howard, 'Morality and Force in International Politics', in *Making Moral Decisions*, ed. D. M. MacKinnon, SPCK 1969.
3. Geoffrey F. Nuttall, *Christianity and Violence*, The F. D. Maurice Lectures for 1970, The Priory Press, Royston 1972.
4. *The Times*, 15 May 1973, for the Court's judgment in the civil action which established incidentally the need for DTI investigation.
5. *The Times*, 17 May 1973.
6. *The Times*, 19 May 1973.
7. See *Personality and Science*, ed. I. T. Ramsey and Ruth Porter, 1971; G. W. E. Wolstenholme and M. O'Connor, *Ethics in Medical Progress*, 1966.
8. *The Times*, 14 October 1969, 1 February 1973.
9. *The Times*, 6 February 1969.
10. *A New Look at the Responsibilities of the British Public Company*, The Confederation of British Industry 1973.
11. Simon Webley, *British Business Men's Behaviour*, Industrial Educational and Research Foundation (now the Foundation for Business Responsibilities) 1971.
12. Simon Webley, *Towards a Code of Business Ethics*, The Christian Association of Business Executives 1972. See Appendix C, 'Codes and Regulation of Behaviour', by Gerard J. Hughes, SJ.
13. See *Man's Wider Loyalties*: Limitations of National Sovereignty [by Vickie Macnair for] The Wyndham Place Trust, Hutchinson 1970.
14. Cf. Michael Howard, op. cit.; Alan R. Booth, *Not Only Peace*, SCM Press 1967.
15. E.g., the Geneva Conventions of 1864, 1906, 1929, 1949; the Hague Conventions of 1899, 1907, 1954; Covenant of the League of Nations, 1919; General Treaty for the Renunciation of War, 1928; United Nations Charter, 1945.
16. For the history see Roland H. Bainton, *Christian Attitudes towards War and Peace*, Hodder and Stoughton 1961; John Eppstein, *The Catholic Tradition of the Law of Nations*, Burns and Oates 1935. For the later development in Christian thought, see Joan D. Tooke, *The Just War in Aquinas and Grotius*, SPCK 1965.

For a summary of the history, especially the later history, and for an account of the 'just war' doctrine in international law, and in the Hague and Geneva Conventions, etc., see Sydney D. Bailey, *Prohibitions and Restraints in War*, Oxford University Press 1972, and 'Can War ever be Humane?', *Theology* LXXV, Nov. 1972, p. 584.

Paul Ramsey's major works in this field are *War and the Christian Conscience*, Duke University Press, Durham, N.C., 1961 and *The Just War: Force and Political Responsibility*, Scribners, New York 1968. For a different treatment see R. T. Osgood and R. W. Tucker, *Force, Order and Justice*, Johns Hopkins Press, Baltimore 1967.

For the 'yellow card', see *The Times*, 1 Feb. 1972, and below, p. 107.

17. See *Theology* LXXIV, March 1971, p. 97, for an editorial review of *Violence in Southern Africa*, a 'Christian Assessment' prepared for the British Council of Churches, SCM Press 1970; see also *The Search for Security*: the Report of a Working Party of the British Council of Churches, SCM Press 1973; *Non-Violent Action*: a Report commissioned for the United Reformed Church, SCM Press 1973; and a review of both by Richard Harries, *Theology* LXXVI, Dec. 1973, pp. 658f.

18. Ramsey, *The Just War*, p. 86.

19. Professor D. H. N. Johnson, of the London School of Economics, in a paper privately circulated.

20. Johnson, op. cit.

21. *The Documents of Vatican II*, ed. Walter M. Abbott, Geoffrey Chapman 1966, p. 294.

22. The International Committee of the Red Cross considered the need for further conventions, especially for the protection of civilians, in internal warfare at its conference in September 1969. *The Times*, 5 Sept. 1969.

23. See the newspapers and Parliamentary Debates for the days following the deaths of 13 civilians in a clash between demonstrators and British troops in Londonderry on Sunday 30 January 1972.

24. Lord Chalfont, *The Times*, 14 May 1973.

25. 'The Legality of Modern Forms of Aerial Warfare', *The Aeronautical Journal of the Royal Aeronautical Society* 72, Aug. 1968, p. 686.

26. The background to the negotiations, stemming from the Geneva protocol of 1925, is traced in Sydney D. Bailey, op. cit., ch. 5. The Biological Weapons Bill, which will enable the UK Government to ratify the Convention, was given a Second Reading in the House of Commons on 21 November 1973.

27. *Chemical and Bacteriological (Biological) Weapons and the Effects of their Possible Use*; New York, the United Nations 1969. Distributed in the UK by HMSO.

28. *The Documents of Vatican II*, the Pastoral Constitution on the Church in the Modern World (*Gaudium et Spes*), ch. V, esp. p. 296.

Index of Subjects

Index of Names